LEAD OR PLEAD

IF YOU CAN LEAD, YOU DON'T NEED TO PLEAD.

DR AMIT DAS

To

All my bosses who made a difference in my professional career.

Great Leaders Thoughts
"Awaken minds.
Bring people together.
Communicate effectively.
Dare to take calculated risks.
Enlighten and empower.
Foster collaboration.
Give you tools to succeed.
Help you do for yourself.
Invite and encourage questions.
Joyfully embrace diversity.
Keep an open mind.
Lead by example.
Motivate with respect.
Never give up on you.
Open doors to new worlds.
Put first things first.
Quest to make learning fun.
Recognize problems early.
Share roles and responsibilities.
Take time to explain things.
Unwrap talents and abilities.
Value everyone's input.
Welcome mistakes as part of learning.
Exceed expectations.
Yearn to connect, not correct.
Zest to make a difference."
- Meiji Stewart, May 2015.

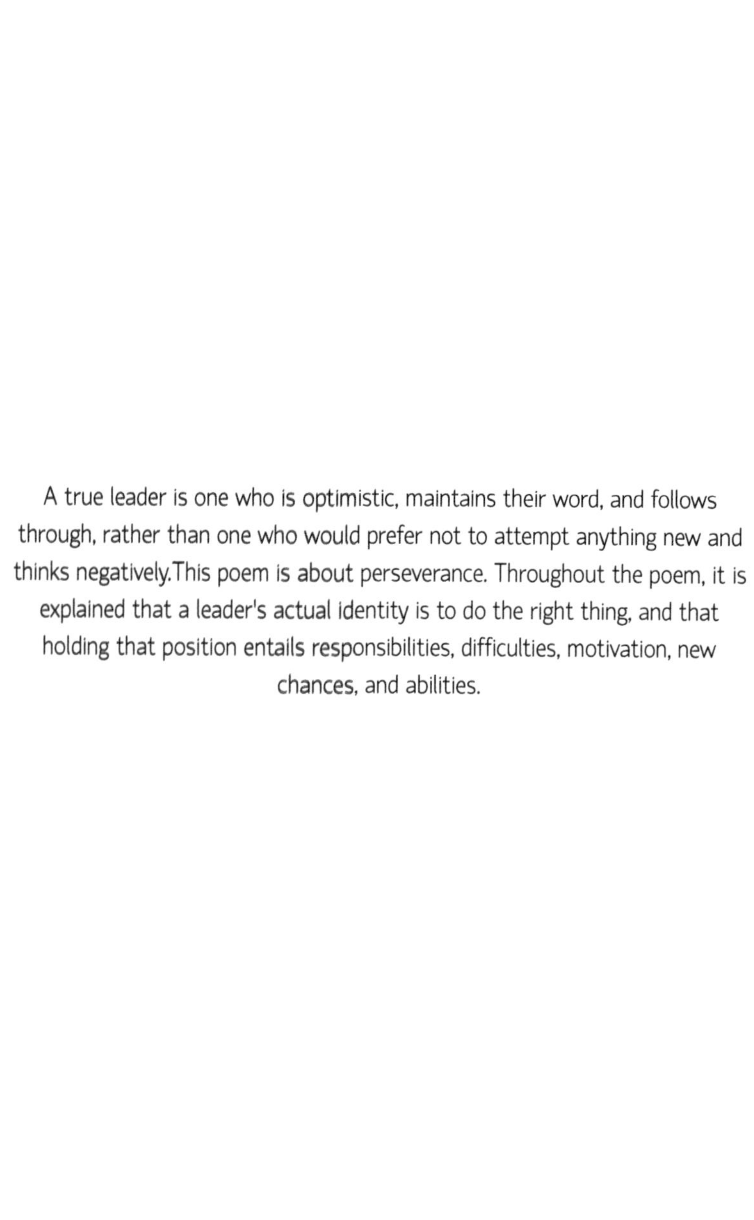

A true leader is one who is optimistic, maintains their word, and follows through, rather than one who would prefer not to attempt anything new and thinks negatively.This poem is about perseverance. Throughout the poem, it is explained that a leader's actual identity is to do the right thing, and that holding that position entails responsibilities, difficulties, motivation, new chances, and abilities.

Contents

Foreword *vii*

Preface *xiii*

Acknowledgements *xxi*

1. Leadership Charisma 1
2. Building Credibility 41
3. Building Trust And Cohesiveness 74
4. Trap Of Perfectionism 93

References 123

About The Author 129

Foreword

"Leadership is a choice, not a position." - Stephen Covey

Dear Readers,

"You aren't optimistic because life is simple. Because life might be difficult, you are optimistic."- Dr. Amit Das, Motivational Speaker and Leadership Coach.

Thank you for taking the time to learn more about leadership capabilities. No one can dream for you, no one can believe in you, and no one can assist you in reaching your objectives. Thank you for taking the time to read this book.

The book *"LEAD OR PLEAD"* is a collection of renowned leaders' footprints and lessons learned. They have had a positive impact on the world via their innovative ideas and tireless efforts. Every person is driven by a desire to lead, inspire, and contribute to the greater good. It might be in your day-to-day duties as a student, or a manager, delegating and managing work in a company. A good leader uses quotations to motivate and inspire his or her followers. You have a leader within you who is always attempting to push the limits and set an example. However, leadership is not a stroll in the park; leaders must possess the traits that will enable them to excel in their particular sectors.

The book *"LEAD OR PLEAD"* describes how to implement the habit of leadership practises into your life to overcome the roadblocks to success, the thieves that steal your energy, and to enhance your dedication to the cause, the way you prioritise, and the productivity of your business. The book is useful for those who work in business or service since it teaches them how to improve their job efficiency and eliminate roadblocks in order to become more successful leaders. The book is easy to read and offers many big topics. The book focuses on how to avoid the confusing hurdles that may appear along the path. By doing so, you will be able to focus on the most essential task at hand. Dr. Amit Das illustrates what makes for great personal and professional leadership with simple but compelling examples and parables from throughout the world. He demonstrates how a natural leadership instinct may be developed while playing any other sport. All of these tales combine to provide an explosive mix that will help you release your inner leader.

The book *"LEAD OR PLEAD"* is intended to assist students, new managers, career changers, and entrepreneurs in learning critical management skills. This book is intended to cover every area of business, from human resources to finance, to marketing to operations, in any sector. Basic basics, key concepts, standard and well-known principles, and practical approaches to applying the subject matter are all covered in this book. The unique feature of this book is that it contains all of the necessary material in a concise and easy-to-understand style.

The book "LEAD OR PLEAD" is the gold-standard guidebook on successful leadership, based on research and published by the field's leading author. With a profound understanding of the workplace's complicated interpersonal dynamics, this book frames leadership as both a talent to be mastered and a relationship to be fostered in order to realise its full potential. This book will teach you how outstanding leaders get remarkable achievements and how to improve your leadership abilities and style so that you can consistently provide high-quality results. In this book you'll learn critical performance and career lessons for managers at all levels, as well as how to apply them to your own position.

Business as usual is gradually losing its efficacy since people work differently, are driven differently, and have different expectations today. In today's workplace, *"LEAD OR PLEAD"* will help you stay current, relevant, and productive. A competent leader gets things done; a great leader wants to do more, encourages others to do more, and accomplish more. This book explains the distinctions between excellent and outstanding, as well as how to bridge the gap between getting things done and getting things done well.

Business is changing at a faster speed than ever before, and CEOs must stay on top or risk stagnation. This high-octane, motivating book on *"LEAD OR PLEAD"* has all of the keys to becoming a visionary leader. The reader will be able to inspire others and build more leaders as a result of reading it. Leadership at all levels is essential for a company's sustainability in business. This book *"LEAD OR PLEAD"*—an internal plan to develop leaders—is either dry or nonexistent. The author illustrates how businesses may develop leadership at every level by identifying prospective leaders, rating their company confidence, structuring their growth, and measuring their accomplishments, based on their experience at several Fortune 500 firms. You will learn extremely essential and practical leadership skills in the most entertaining and refreshing way possible in this book. Read gripping leadership stories that range from corporate drama to suspense. There are significant, practical, and application-based leadership ideas hidden inside these stories. This book includes transformative leadership teachings for everyone, whether you are an aspiring or seasoned leader in your community or the business sector, or even if you are a CEO.

The book *"LEAD OR PLEAD"* offers an alternative to traditional leadership by focusing on leading via inspiration rather than control. This is an excellent manual for prospective and current leaders alike, with many practical examples that provide leaders with reference points for navigating their own company attitude, associations, and career. Dr. Amit Das, an expert at finding pain areas, has left no stone unturned in softly and frankly confronting the issues at hand. His plain-spoken demeanour will appeal to managers on the job, as it has in his previous consulting jobs. It is a strong and instructive book that should be thumbed through frequently and in real time. This book is a must-read for young leaders who desire to achieve their given responsibilities. It gives enormous value in terms of coaching and growth. The return in terms of results will be great for all those leaders who extract the lessons from this simple yet powerful book. The insights from this book present a vision of linked-leadership—leaders who are linked through loving-connection with themselves (through self-knowledge), with other beings, with nature, and with the supreme source, especially in these times when there is a crisis of faith in leadership. This book's unique insights will help you understand different personality types and encourage others based on their natural tendencies, which will aid you in developing productive teams and creating a peaceful and lucrative corporate culture.

In this book you'll hear first-hand tales from some of the most successful organizational leaders in recent history, from SBI's Chairman to Pepsico's CEO, as they reveal how their distinctive characteristics have fueled their success as you read this leadership book. This book *"LEAD OR PLEAD"* will provide you with a fresh road map for guiding people toward a better future, filled with cutting-edge research and concrete ideas. The book*"LEAD OR PLEAD"* focuses on the genuine obstacles and possibilities you face throughout your professional life. This book gives inspiration and guidance for tackling challenges at work, such as unfairness, promotion, and community building, through interviews and relevant articles, tales, and research. This book will help you start crucial conversations about where you are now and how to move forward by providing thorough discussion tips. This book clearly demonstrates how a leader can teach individuals to bring out the best in them and how coaching can release creativity and innovation while encouraging teams to reach their full potential. It also looks at how coaching may help leaders strike a balance between controlling and directing their teams, as well as appraising and supporting them. While there are many outstanding books on leadership, talent, and coaching, this is a rare book that boldly stands at the confluence of leadership and coaching.

This book *"LEAD OR PLEAD"* will show you all of the qualities that distinguish exceptional leaders from the others. These leadership qualities can help you pave the way, whether you're seeking a promotion, a new company endeavour, or simply a new direction in your life. Each skill is thoroughly taught so that you can apply it to your own life and see how it all fits together. This book explains how this might occur and where you should begin. The characteristics presented in the book are those that distinguish ordinary individuals. This isn't the book for you if you'd rather turn the other way and keep doing what you're doing. If you're tired of watching others reap the benefits, this book will show you the attributes you'll need and explain them in a way that you can grasp, putting you on the road to success. This book "*LEAD OR PLEAD*" delves into the new methods and attitudes required of today's next-generation leaders. The book provides suggestions to help leaders excite their teams in ways that a paycheck never could.

This book "*LEAD OR PLEAD*" uses the framework for examining multiple aspects of personal leadership effectiveness: individual desire, their identity, their dignity, self- motivation, and their indomitable ambition. The author claims that leaders are blinded by power and control, construct their own performance treadmill, live for the favour of others, and have myopic objectives because they are preoccupied with themselves . The leadership concepts discussed in the book, as well as their street-level applications, are based on academic research, and will empower both rookie and seasoned leaders to start and finish successfully. In a nutshell, this book challenges and prepares leaders to stand up and promote unity and diversity in their businesses in order to attain long-term well-being and enjoyment.

So, happy reading and learning to all my readers.

Carpe diem.

Dr. Amit Das

Preface

"Leadership is not a popularity contest; it's about leaving your ego at the door. The name of the game is to lead without a title." - Robin S. Sharma

Businesses are now operating in a VUCA (volatile, unpredictable, complex, and ambiguous) environment. This new reality has caused firms to shift away from traditional command-and-control techniques and toward an entirely new paradigm, one in which leaders encourage and assist their employees. In a digital and disruptive age, the challenges of governance, leadership, and HR provide a road map for leadership that is all about turning adversity into an opportunity for transformation. This book provides a path ahead for transformative leadership in Indian banks through an exceptional combination of papers, case studies, and interviews. Despite their great accomplishments, public sector banks confront a number of obstacles, including rising non-performing assets, shrinking market share, and low market capitalization. This book argues for a fundamental shift in the structure and process of governance, including board-level autonomy, CEO tenure and compensation, people process, talent development, and building a leadership pipeline, to make banks resilient, strong, and future-proof in the face of competition and digitalization, which necessitate new business models.

This new reality has caused firms to abandon traditional command-and-control tactics in favour of a whole new paradigm in which executives encourage and guide their team members rather than instruct and manage them. Leadership coaching examines some of the major components of good leadership and provides advice based on research and in-depth analysis on how to become an effective leader-coach. The book is a light read, peppered with entertaining tales and parallels culled from athletics, the performing arts, and other areas of life. Interviews with business executives and academics round out the story. This book will be valuable to leaders, aspiring leaders, and especially those who aspire to shift from being good to great leaders.

Who knows what it takes to be a successful leader in today's world?

The most successful CEOs may learn essential lessons on the most important components of leadership from the brains of India's top CEOs. Even the most accomplished leaders have to find their leadership calling and develop their attributes with intentional effort and practise, according to this collection of brief personal accounts from legendary corporate executives. The majority of leadership literature is very formal and instructional. However, leadership is not and never will be a one-size-fits-all idea. This book arose from a desire to study the art of leadership through the most successful leaders' distinctive examples. This book guides the reader through the path of these executives from unremarkable individuals to famous business giants, allowing them to take inspiration and learn from their trials and accomplishments.

Have you ever pondered why some people seem to be successful while your life seems to be stuck in a rut? The fact is that you have the same opportunities as everyone else; you simply haven't figured out how to take advantage of them. This book teaches you that you can do everything you set your mind to, and that having the appropriate leadership abilities will help you steer your life in the correct direction. There are a lot of people that live boring lives. They might have a lot of experience. They may be able to make a decent income, but how many of them truly live their dream? You can turn your life around and go in the correct direction if you have the appropriate abilities. It's only a question of changing your expectations.

If you identify yourself in any of the following scenarios:

- *Are you new to managing teams and unsure of how to motivate and lead people that rely on you?*
- *Don't you wish you had a personal mentor to assist you with these and other frequent leadership issues?*

- *Do you find it difficult to manage your team during periods of upheaval and volatility?*
- *Are you interested in learning more about how to grow as a leader and live a more fulfilling life and career?*

When you combine your expertise and insights with storytelling, you get thought-starters to help you uncover solutions to typical difficulties faced by new leaders. It's a self-help book that primarily speaks about gaining success in life, pointing out what one needs in order to thrive in both personal and professional lives. These aren't extensive theories or sophisticated models, but basic, easy, and practical counsel based on Dr. Amit Das's two-and-a-half decades of business experience and the wisdom of the many wonderful teachers he's had along the way. This is your own mentor, one that you can carry with you! Addressing your leadership difficulties with simple, byte-sized answers—one hundred words at a time—this is your personal mentor, one that you can carry with you!

To be a successful leader, one must not only do an outstanding job but also successfully express his or her ideas as a great speaker. Great leaders have complete confidence in their actions and judgments. They recognize the importance and power of their words. The author's deep grasp of human psychology allows him to help his readers make the best and most successful choices in life. The current book, *" LEAD OR PLEAD,"* provides readers with the skills necessary to give successful and impassioned speeches, and it aids in the development of exceptional leaders.

It doesn't matter what you do in business; what matters is *"why"* and *"how"* you do it. The author demonstrates how firms may evolve beyond understanding what they do to knowing how they do it, and then ask the more crucial question, *"How would I make it?"* Learning to ask good questions is the key to running a successful business. Examples and ideas from global leaders and organizations can assist you in finding solutions and a path ahead. Boost your leadership abilities by experiencing the incredible power of wearing a lens of wealth, curiosity, and intent. His goal is to make this an easy-to-read and pleasurable experience by blending his real-life experiences of over 22 years, interviews with great executives across sectors, and a useful resource bank.

According to the book, one wants to be successful in their everyday lives, whether professional or personal, in order to pay attention to the most essential things. Similarly, higher productivity is desired in order for one's work to grow. According to the book, one desires both less and more at the same time, and this may be obtained by employing particular techniques. The book assists in reducing leadership mistakes, igniting one's drive to become excited in their activities focused on their goals, overcoming feelings of tiredness caused by overwhelming occurrences, and achieving greater accomplishments in less time.

Have you ever wondered how to become the kind of person who people seek for advice?

In this book, you will discover what it takes to be a great leader who can lead any team to success. This straightforward handbook, based on the most recent leadership research, breaks down not just the attributes of highly effective leaders but also how to use those skills in a range of scenarios. You don't have to be in a position of leadership to benefit from the teachings in this book. The book analyses the finest practises of effective leadership and the essential abilities of powerful leaders, in addition to outlining the ideas of leadership and motivation. It also provides insight into real-world issues that successful businesses have faced and solved.

In this intriguing book, you'll discover the essential characteristics that distinguish the best-of-the-best firms (those in the top quartile) from the other three-quarters of the pack. You'll learn about the dumb things managers do to sabotage greatness in the workplace, as well as what can be done to correct those errors and move into a constructive leadership role. Read on if you're a forward-thinking leader who recognizes that you won't be able to achieve your full leadership potential without the devotion and loyalty of engaged people.

What if you could learn the secrets of revolutionary and exponential growth?

Encourage employees to be more engaged and loyal. Can you increase your chances of success by cultivating trust in your relationships? Can you be a standout performer by dealing with adversity? Be a winner in all of your goals by thinking bigger, doing bigger, and being bigger. How can you boost your happiness quotient by winning and collaborating? Can you create a strategy plan for realising your company's vision? extend your horizons and attain goals that are outside of your comfort zone? create a more productive and rewarding workplace. Personal growth and transformation rarely occur *"by chance,"* but rather as a result of your deliberate decisions. This book provides strong personal change principles gathered from the lives of renowned leaders. It provides you with essential guidance on how to live a more enlightened life, one that is more purposeful, purpose-driven, self-aware, and socially responsible. The author uses language that is straightforward, colourful, and extremely entertaining to describe and illustrate each of these lessons, drawing on a variety of subjects such as psychology, business, leadership, philosophy, and spirituality. These lessons are founded on timeless truths that, when properly pondered and integrated into your everyday lives, may profoundly alter you while having a good influence on the world. The book is both a practical manual and a contribution to the continuing discussion about what sort of leadership you should be promoting in today's chaotic and uncertain environment, which is amidst current worldwide concerns about leadership quality.

Leadership and change go hand in hand, yet the essential building blocks of leadership stay the same during times of transition. Lessons in Leadership provides direction, inspiration, comfort, and insight regardless of the size of the team to be led—whether it is 10 or 10,000 people. This book is the result of a 22-year accumulation of experiences. Leading voices from the worlds of business, politics, and education will be needed to help mankind progress to a better world tomorrow, as selfless leaders dedicated to making a difference may inject ideas for future generations. This book is a collection of reflections for young aspiring leaders to study and absorb in order to help them discover a higher route to improve humanity's growth.

This is a great resource for executives who want to achieve high performance while maintaining their integrity. With a few basic tools, you can completely transform your workplace. This remarkable book provides surprising and amazing solutions to difficult leadership questions like:

- *How can you better serve your customers by serving your people?*
- *How can you reconcile your own views with your leadership job in a way that feels good 'deep down' while still achieving the required outcomes?*
- *How can you lead with integrity and obtain customers who appreciate the service, employees who enjoy their jobs, and financial well-being?*

By evaluating messaging, the authors provide basic ways for bringing vision—and values—to the workplace. This book is a series of reflections on the principles of leadership aimed at challenging and inspiring the reader. It is for anybody interested in learning more about the ideas and difficulties surrounding leadership as a management function.

Employees want and need to feel that their efforts are valued. Gratitude is the simplest, quickest, and least expensive strategy to improve employee performance. According to a new study, appreciation increases employee engagement, lowers turnover, and encourages team members to express thanks to one another, so it builds team relationships. Gratitude is also advantageous to people who express it, according to research, and is one of the most potent predictors of a person's overall well-being, surpassing money, health, and optimism. The firm achieved historic sales growth after the leadership trained thousands of managers on how to demonstrate thanks to their staff.

The theme of the book is all those leaders who were not respected in their traditional domains, but whose philosophies proved them wrong. This book, which emphasises that everyone can be a leader, is written in the form of a business story, which makes it all the more exciting and engaging. Each talk focuses on a few key themes that will assist ordinary individuals in becoming genuine leaders and achieving positions in their businesses. The book is aimed at managers and students who wish to develop their leadership abilities. It provides a basic overview of leadership styles and boosts your capacity to identify where you stand as a leader.It's a handbook that has the potential to bring the globe together in terms of corporate leadership and human interaction. This book is a valuable resource that provides new ideas, insights, and inspiration that have the potential to change the way people lead. Let's get this priceless instrument into the hands of the appropriate people-yours!

The author offers you simple frameworks give a primer for individuals seeking continual development; by internalising important ideas and putting them into action, you'll become a more successful and influential leader. You, the Leader, address the challenges you'll experience on your way to the top, such as not getting credit for your efforts, feeling invisible, and being subjected to unfair prejudices and expectations. This book will help you better grasp how to remain honest while demonstrating yourself as a recognized leader in your business with guidance, recommendations, and realistic dialogues. Struggling to prioritise between results and people; wondering if you have *"leadership genes"* or if you were even meant to be a leader; insufficient authority to lead and drive change not knowing how to inspire people. unable to effectively listen, coach, delegate, lead meetings, or drive higher performance;facing challenges in developing team spirit and collaboration among your people; finding it difficult to engage people and align them with the organization's goals; finding it difficult to engage people and align them with the organization's goals. This book will help you remember why you lead, why and how to be inspired, and how to inspire others. This is your go-to leadership resource. The author drew on the experiences of thousands of CEOs from across the world to produce a clear action plan that can be applied to any business. Executive leadership is the key to a company's quality revolution—and to creating the actual cost savings that improved quality provides in the short and long run, according to this crucial manual.

Acknowledgements

At the outset I will thank to my family for supporting me throughout the journey of writing my book and encouraging me to live my dreams- my son has always been instrumental in giving his inspiration to complete the writing of this book. Despite the fact that I am listed as the author of this book, "BYPB" would not have been published if I had depended entirely on my own talents. To create this book required more than a village—it took a family of dedicated and caring people who were always prepared to lend a hand.

Writing a book while working full-time is no simple task, so I'd want to express my gratitude to my amazing coworkers, who act as mentors and cheerleaders in equal measure. Thank you, too, to the rest of the accumentor team for your patience and unflinching support while I worked on this book!

Thank you to everyone who has listened to me argue for doing everything you can to make your life, including your work life, more progressive. I appreciate everyone's assistance throughout the process. This book would not have been possible without each of you having had an impact on my life in some manner.

Lastly, I would like to thank all the people whom I have been associated, you gave me power. I would like to thank Notion Press for publishing my book. At last thank you all for gifting your time to read out this book.

I'd want to convey my heartfelt appreciation to the almighty god for bestowing his blessings and being so gracious.

CHAPTER ONE

LEADERSHIP CHARISMA

How Do People Perceive Their Captivating Leadership Strengths?

"Before you are a leader, success is all about growing yourself. When you become a leader, success is all about growing others." - Jack Welch

Businesses, like civilizations, experience ups and downs. Similarly, some leaders remain in power for decades while others fade away after only a few years. Great leaders, on the other hand, do not come into power with a silver spoon in their mouth or a vast economic fortune. Business executives' sheer perseverance and enthusiasm pave the path for new chances and bigger projects. There are various characteristics that distinguish a successful business leader, including the ability to motivate people and the ability to articulate a clear vision that others can believe in. Excellent leadership is the only way to create long-term success. Leadership is a set of abilities that can be learned and practised, not a mystical talent. Not everyone can be a great leader, but everyone can improve their leadership skills. It may come more naturally to some, but it is not inaccessible to others.

Researchers have been striving to understand if a great leader is born with inherent leadership abilities or if a person can be trained and developed into a leader.

Leadership, according to the latest scientific studies, is 30% hereditary and 70% learned. According to these findings, leaders are developed rather than born. The finest leaders require a strong set of leadership abilities to connect with their employees, colleagues, and clients, and there are various programmes that may help you become a visionary leader.

"It doesn't matter when we start. It doesn't matter where we start. All that matters is that we start." - Simon Sinek

Leadership abilities are vital, whether one is operating a business, managing a team, or teaching a class. Every company will face adversity at some point, and although executives must make difficult decisions about how to improve their condition, they must also pay special attention to staff morale. Low spirits frequently cause the most damage to a company. The term *"leadership"* is a very broad and ambiguous one. *"The action of leading"* and/or *"a person who controls, directs, or inspires others"* are two commonly recognized definitions of leadership.

According to these criteria, anyone may be a leader, whether they formally manage and lead a team as a manager or supervisor, or whether they just find themselves in a position to influence others.

Today's technical leaders are expected to demonstrate better commercial acumen, as well as the correct blend of people and business skills, as well as other interpersonal qualities. In modern enterprizes, technology has an undeniable consistency. In the next few years, the many scopes of technology leadership positions will continue to change and extend to meet the changing market needs, consumer landscape, technical discoveries, security standards, and business requirements. Companies that are tech-driven recognize the importance and purpose of technological breakthroughs and innovations, making it simpler for them to accept the change in tech leadership positions. In reality, technological developments are affecting organizational tendencies, so you may expect a lot of dynamism in tech leadership jobs in 2021 and beyond.

"Leadership is solving problems. The day soldiers stop bringing you their problems is the day you have stopped leading them. They have either lost confidence that you can help or conclude you do not care. Either case is a failure of leadership." - Colin Powell

As a leader, you'll have to deal with a lot of challenges, hostility, and difficulties. There may be times when it appears as if the entire universe is conspiring against you, and your vision appears to be a work of fiction rather than reality. That is why it is critical to have positive leadership! Positive leadership isn't about feigning happiness. It is the genuine substance that distinguishes outstanding leaders. The evidence is indisputable. It's not merely a pleasant way to lead to be a positive leader. If you want to create a strong culture, unify your business in the face of adversity, generate a connected and devoted workforce, and achieve greatness and success, this is the way to lead. Positive leadership has a lot of power, and you can start using it to help yourself and your team right now.

"For the success of any mission, it is necessary to have leadership. Leadership is vital for government, non-governmental organizations as well as industries."

Jack Ma was the first mainland Chinese entrepreneur to appear on the cover of Forbes magazine. He is also the founder of the Alibaba Group, a digital conglomerate who emerged from humble beginnings to become a global role model for other entrepreneurs. Jack Ma had been rejected from university three times before being accepted to Hangzhou Teacher's Institute. He applied for 30 jobs after graduation and was turned down for each one. During a short journey to the United States, he first learned about the internet, and when he came home, he developed a little website about China and Chinese items. This would be his first move toward founding a corporation that would set the world record for the largest initial public offering (IPO).

"No matter how tough the chase is, you should always have the dream you saw on the first day. It'll keep you motivated and rescue you (from any weak thoughts). " —Jack Ma

Jack has amassed a fortune of over a billion dollars via his own efforts. His transformation from English teacher to e-commerce tycoon may make for a compelling case study at business schools. In this regard, let's talk about the lessons he's learned as a leader. He had the benefit of time and timing on his side. The internet was flourishing when he started working in the industry. His ability to communicate in English helped him investigate business options outside of China. To launch his e-commerce firm, he efficiently used the English language and the internet's timeliness. David Hsu, a Wharton professor of management, emphasized three characteristics that distinguish Jack Ma.

1. His early understanding of the entrepreneur potential , taking it, and constructing the vision and firm to execute it in the face of a highly complex business environment.

2. He has carved an alternative professional route for many Chinese rather than the tried-and-true paradigm. He's not afraid to admit his mistakes. He's been tenacious in his pursuit of many chances, and he's had to forge his own path.

3. Rather than resting on the Alibaba legacy, retiring early and aspiring to do something new to keep his mind engaged and to enter a different sector than what he's in. Here are a few takeaways from his leadership.

"A leader should have more grit and tenacity, and be able to endure what the employees can't." —Jack Ma

Jack Ma employs individuals who are brighter than he is. He educates and grooms them in accordance with the company's culture and needs. In his work, he emphasizes the significance of attitude and enthusiasm above theoretical knowledge.

"Complaining should be avoided. Successful individuals, seldom grumble." Jack Ma

You are upbeat and work well with others. Make the most of your time by looking into business options. You made blunders when it came to seeking funds. You made blunders in management. In HR, you committed blunders. Failures are a great way to learn. The government did not assist Jack Ma in any way. He raised money from the stock market and other sources, particularly consumers. To his shareholders and consumers, he demonstrated higher returns. His customers began to like and admire him. He prefers to be respected over loved. Educate and train the next generation of leaders. They create possibilities for citizens and government officials. Encourage people to succeed in the world. Make others stronger by empowering them. Jack Ma is a business aficionado. He has made up his mind. He is a firm believer in collaboration. Customers come first, staff second, and stockholders third, according to him. He embraces change and places a premium on attaining achievement while maintaining integrity.

"We made more mistakes than anyone would fathom." -Jack Ma

Leadership is always there at the tipping moment to alter the world for the better. However, history has shown that even the most powerful leaders are vulnerable to derailment and failure. The prevalent belief that leaders must improve their self-efficacy in order to be effective is incorrect, because the self is the heart of the leadership problem. You already know that good leaders must be aware of their own emotions as well as those around them.

"The supreme quality for leadership is unquestionably integrity. Without it, no real success is possible, no matter whether it is on a section gang, a football field, in an army, or in an office."- Dwight D. Eisenhower

Emotional intelligence is no longer a *"nice to have"* characteristic; it is now mission-critical. These abilities were put to the test during the epidemic. In challenging situations and at all times, creating a compassionate work atmosphere where workers feel respected as people and can openly express their ideas and concerns is critical. Leaders must be open and honest about their expectations in order to foster and sustain a culture of trust. Employee engagement is really higher when leadership communicates with them frequently and freely.

Without corner offices, leaders who do not inspire their staff do not deserve their titles. That will be much clearer in 2022. Real leaders acquire respect by listening to their subordinates, providing counsel, and advocating vehemently when the situation demands it. Leadership in 2022 will be straightforward, with less pomp and circumstance. The era of stale leadership theories has come to an end. The dawn of a new era of trust, honesty, and personal initiative has arrived.

"Effective leadership is not about making speeches or being liked; leadership is defined by results, not attributes." - Peter F. Drucker

Preparing for anything also entails being open to anything, and what better way to do it than by exchanging ideas? Leaders aren't flawless, and they need help from time to time. More importantly, they must be receptive to new ideas that may benefit the entire company, even if they did not originate with them. Moving forward, it will be even more critical to develop leaders that are open to any proposal from anyplace, have no ego or agenda, and prioritise the health of the company and its employees. Despite the numerous obstacles of the past few years, they have also inspired your collective human spirit and revealed your genuine grit.

- *Do you find it difficult to lead at times?*
- *Do you ever find yourself in a power struggle?*
- *Is it possible that you are your own worst critic?*

Then this straightforward guide to effective leadership and management is for you. The fear of trying new things is the worst. Create a good work environment. Assist your team in achieving a shared objective. Enjoy the road to leadership mastery with your team. Consider your options carefully. Boost your productivity and performance.

LinkedIn's CEO is Jeff Weiner. Despite the fact that LinkedIn was created in 2002, it was under Weiner's leadership that the company completed its initial public offering (IPO) and became one of the world's most popular social networking platforms. He describes himself as *"compassion-driven,"* but it wasn't always that way — and without a pivotal discussion, he would not have been able to propel LinkedIn to a multibillion-dollar IPO and, subsequently, a Microsoft purchase.

"The important word there is inspire. The key difference between managers and leaders is that managers tell people what to do, while leaders inspire them to do it. Inspiration comes from three things: clarity of one's vision, courage of their conviction, and the ability to effectively communicate both of those things."

He possesses the skills needed to construct and enhance company strategies as a graduate of the University of Pennsylvania's Wharton School. Of course, classroom knowledge does not necessarily translate to real-world success. Execution, developing relationships, and understanding how to keep people motivated to achieve mutual goals are all important aspects of business success.

"The more people you're responsible for, the more your words and the way you communicate those words, your body language, and essentially everything you do is taken into consideration by the team."

Jeff Weiner's leadership style does not neatly fall into any one category. He's developed a unique technique over the years. He believes that developing a successful, real leadership style involves time, effort, and practice. If the leader isn't inspired, no one else on the team will be either. Weiner's enthusiasm is contagious. When he talks about LinkedIn's future, for example, you start to become excited about the possibilities. Good leaders must be aware of their surroundings, including the status of the industry, the company's assets, areas for improvement, and developing technologies that may open up new business prospects. You are not required to work for him or one of his businesses. The topic is noteworthy because of its inner source of motivation.Weiner uses the term *"consciousness"* in a broad sense that incorporates a variety of attributes. Leaders must also be conscious that they are in charge. This may appear to be self-evident, yet it is actually extremely smart. How many CEOs focus on completing tasks without contemplating the impact of their behavior on those around them? They have positions of leadership, yet they don't necessarily consider themselves to be leaders. Instead, they get so preoccupied with getting things done that they forget to maintain a cheerful, upbeat demeanor toward everyone in business.

"You have to feel it deeply to be able to overcome those challenges and for people to want to follow you. And if you're not authentic in that belief and you don't have true conviction, they're not going to be behind you. "

Weiner appears to be a transformative leader in that he creates a vision, communicates it, and inspires others to achieve their objectives. He gives employees and supervisors an opportunity to succeed. He also provides them with chances to fall short of their objectives. Falling short isn't always a failure. It's a chance to learn more about what works and what doesn't in one's working life. Transformational leadership has several advantages. Employee turnover is reduced, and employees are more happy in their positions. It also places a high priority on interpersonal interactions. Weiner is willing to collaborate with others in order to achieve a common aim. Weiner believes that leaders must be aware of the synthesis of technology and possibilities available to them. They can't live in bubbles, isolated from the rest of the world. Instead, they must stay on the leading edge of new trends. Weiner wants to be able to see all that is going on around him so that he can make educated decisions that will move his organization and employees ahead.

"You have to maintain a culture of transformation and stay true to your values."

Leaders can only make gut choices without synthesis. That strategy has worked for several great leaders. However, in today's world of corporate intelligence and analytics, the *"gut instinct"* concept is becoming less and less relevant.

"Outstanding leaders go out of their way to boost the self-esteem of their personnel. If people believe in themselves, it's amazing what they can accomplish."- Sam Walton

When leaders consider the future and where work will be done, the option should not be viewed as binary, with everyone either returning to the status quo or performing 100% telework. A more adaptable workplace for a workforce that can work from anywhere yet is empowered to work from their most productive location might be the best option. To understand how—and why—to build adaptive workplaces, top officials should reconsider what productivity means. Economists generally define productivity as outputs divided by inputs. In this example, boosting productivity involves lowering the number of workers needed to produce widgets.

The ultimate crash course in flexibility has been navigating the corporate landscape in the midst of a pandemic. Reprioritizing became a crucial talent for effective leadership while dealing with halted and cancelled contracts, reinvented and fully new services, organisational restructuring, and brand new technology. Leaders couldn't wait for something unexpected to happen next. They have to constantly innovate and anticipate. Only 12% of firms had contingency plans in place when the pandemic first struck, indicating that they were not well prepared. Covid had strewn fragments throughout many elements of its company operations, leaving many racing to pick up the pieces. In the aftermath of such a massive incident that has influenced many aspects of life, the company leader must be prepared to plan for the short-, mid-, and long-term. They must have a keener eye for opportunity, the capacity to adjust to changing circumstances, and the willingness to take on new challenges.

To see results and retain their personal well-being, leaders must separate *"need-to-do"* chores from *"not-as-necessary"* tasks. 2022 was a year for separating busy from driven, with the awareness that the latter was far more essential. As organisations confront new problems in the post-Covid era, this freshly developed capacity to fast prioritize will be critical, and having a CEO who can do so will distinguish enterprizes that favour conscious work over continual work.

"I think one of the keys to leadership is recognizing that everybody has gifts and talents. A good leader will learn how to harness those gifts toward the same goal." - Ben Carson

Improvisation is a kind of leadership. You can be guided by an overarching purpose, strong beliefs, and a strategic plan, but what you do in the moment cannot be premeditated. You must react as events unfold. To use your metaphor, you must move from the balcony to the dance floor on a daily, weekly, monthly, and annual basis. While today's approach may appear sensible at the moment, tomorrow you'll discover unforeseen repercussions of today's actions and will need to adjust your strategy appropriately. Successful leadership requires, first and foremost, the capacity to observe and comprehend what is occurring to you and your enterprise in real time.

Leaders are made; they are not born. They are made by hard effort, which is the price that all of us must pay to achieve any goal that is worthwhile. - Vince Lombardi

Leaders in high-performing teams create a sense of urgency and purpose. Leaders are used to dealing with complexity, instability, and change. They have the ability to mobilize the organization in the face of adversity. Imaginative leaders are needed, but they cannot be lone wolves or independent operators; the heroic corporate leader's days are numbered. Today's leaders must work collaboratively with their peers and recognize the collective power that comes from working together. They'll have to deal with more outsiders in the future, such as nonprofit organizations, regulators, and other agencies that are more active in business.

Future leaders with skills that are relevant to future needs are on the way. Rotating between various types of roles and responsibilities in various departments and areas has helped to develop leaders in high-performance firms. These organisations identify and nurture future leaders at an early stage in their careers. The finest leaders require a strong set of leadership abilities to connect with their employees, colleagues, and clients, and there are various programmes that may help you become a visionary leader. Being a leader is like riding a violent roller coaster with many ups and downs, twists and turns. And it's during those low points that you search for motivation to keep going. It happens frequently; in fact, it occurs on a regular basis.

" Integrity, insight, and inclusiveness are the essential qualities of leadership."

The "Five Cs," as the author refers to his list of critical leadership skills,

- Competency (becoming known as the term for a specific expertise)
- Courage (be willing to speak up and out)
- Critical communication skills (delivering tough messages)
- Collaboration (creating a coherent work culture)
- Compassionate (Showing empathy to build a winning team)

"Leadership is about empathy. It is about having the ability to relate to and connect with people for the purpose of inspiring and empowering their lives."- Oprah Winfrey

Empathy has been highlighted as a top leadership talent for the modern leader, but leaders must go beyond merely knowing empathy to actively cultivating it in order to help their team achieve their objectives. Empathetic leaders guide employees through all of this to help them achieve their full potential. Let's start by defining what empathy is and isn't. Empathy is the ability to sense, feel, understand, and relate to the feelings and thoughts of others. Empathy is not compassion or experiencing another's sentiments of bereavement with pity as the primary emotion. Empathy is about making people feel seen and heard, and it's about letting them know they're not alone. It isn't about addressing other people's issues. So now that you know what empathy is, let's go to work on getting results.

Crisis And Uncertainty

Crises cause a lot of commotion. It has the potential to be extremely dangerous for individuals. The most important factor is that you do not feel secure. The element of emotion is one of the defining characteristics of a crisis. As a result, a crisis will put you to the test. People will be listening intently to whatever you say. Everyone is staring at you. If you're in the midst of a crisis, it's critical to take a moment to catch your breath. Correct, you must first manage your emotions before you can begin to obtain knowledge. So, as a leader, how can you ensure that your team is safe? Your team needs something to aim for and strive for, as well as the assurance that they can succeed even if things don't appear to be going well.

So, during a crisis, change is frequently coming at your team at a breakneck pace, and they're feeling overwhelmed. Furthermore, you are physiologically programmed to resist change. As a result, you're naturally programmed to see every prospective change as a danger. When you are agitated by change, you go through a process known as the *"change curve."* You go through a series of emotions, starting with being upset. You're annoyed, disappointed, and perplexed. And when you move through those feelings, you eventually come to accept them and look forward to them. The negative feelings, on the other hand, occur on the front side. And I constantly advise leaders that their employees aren't trying to be tough. They're just being themselves. It's a part of it.

"Build resilience in yourselves. When tragedy or disappointment strike, know that you have the ability to get through absolutely anything. I promise you do. As the saying goes, we are more vulnerable than we ever thought, but we are stronger than we ever imagined."-Sheryl Sandberg

To live, to belong, and to become the best version of yourself. To be the first to live That's your basic need for food, water, and shelter, and it's understandable if you're in a crisis, but it's also your new need to do well at work. Your ability to have stable employment. The second factor is your want to belong, to be a member of a community, to be a part of a group that you care about and that cares about you, which for most of you is your family and coworkers. As a result, anything that threatens people's sense of belonging or prevents them from being together will elicit strong reactions. The third point is that you're predisposed to it.

For many leaders, difficult talks, those exchanges that keep you up at night, are a typical difficulty. Wouldn't it be great if you could approach difficult situations without becoming worried, losing sleep, or continuously rehearsing what-if scenarios? Fortunately, this is doable, and the first step should be to prepare. In this session, I'll show you how to prepare for the meeting so that you can have a productive conversation. Begin by identifying the meeting's business goal and expected outcome. Why are you having this conversation and what do you want to happen as a result? Discussing the cancellation of a project and how it affects an employee and their work is an example of a purpose, or why.

You're all on a path of learning, developing, and improving, and anything that comes in the way might truly agitate you and make you upset. So these things will serve you well as a leader no matter what's going on, but during a crisis, remember that these things are on high alert, and where you can help people feel safe and secure, where you can help them feel connected and part of a community, and where you can help them learn and grow through what's going on, that will tick all the boxes on their biological makeup and needs.

"A leader is like a shepherd. He stays behind the flock, letting the most nimble go out ahead, whereupon the others follow, not realizing that all along, they are being directed from behind."- Nelson Mandela

Individuals are naturally resistant to change, this can make the whole problem even more dramatic and distressing for them. So that's one component of your aversion to change. Another question is whether you had the opportunity to select the change and whether you desired it. People have a difficult time becoming enthused about change that they either didn't desire or didn't have a say in. And leaders can do a lot to mitigate this by including others, talking about the problem you're tackling, and soliciting their feedback. Because if they get the opportunity to talk about it and buy into it, they will.

So, clearly, leaders can prepare individuals for this by offering training, creating opportunities for practise, and just having patience. It takes time for people to work through their emotions and frustrations and build new behaviours. Things get easier and people become happier as a result. If there's one thing you can do to help your team embrace change, it's to acknowledge that it's up to you. It's your job to create a conducive environment for them to succeed. As a result, you must be precise and consistent in your communication. It entails showing compassion and understanding for the emotional process they're going through and preparing them for a successful trip.

"Leaders think and talk about the solutions. Followers think and talk about the problems." - Brian Tracy

Most leaders make the error of announcing a change and then expecting their followers to figure it out on their own. They also refuse to accept responsibility for ensuring the success of the entire event. So, when a crisis occurs, it's critical for the leader to find a way to remain cool since so many others will be looking to you to offer that sense of strength and confidence so that they don't panic. As a result, when you role model it as a leader, you're not just becoming a better leader because you're calmer, but you're also giving others permission to do it as well. And, as much as you may speak the words, don't be concerned.

"Leadership is not bullying and leadership is not aggression. Leadership is the expectation that you can use your voice for good. That you can make the world a better place."

Well, I believe there are crucial things to remember while reacting to a crisis. The first is that you must communicate with a specific goal in mind. So, if you need to slow down a little to make sure you've thought through your replies and have a strategy, do so first, because people will be listening intently to everything you say. As a result, you should be very deliberate in your communications and ensure that they have a purpose. The second point to remember is to be as open as possible. Lack of knowledge will agitate people's biology of survival.

You want to be completely open about what you know, when you know it, why things are occurring, and when you'll be able to provide them with further details. You want your communication to be the foundation on which they may now rely. You'll also feel like a broken record since you'll communicate more than you've ever communicated before.

You may have a handful of people with whom you feel comfortable venting and processing your feelings. Then there's the possibility that you merely want to lean on your team or family, but you want to respect your sentiments. You don't want to bury them or force them down because they will resurface. But what you want to do is digest things and get in shape so that you can come out and truly feel like you've got this and emanate that presence so that others believe it and can depend on you. The fourth thing you should do is focus on empathy and compassion. Crises agitate everyone's emotions. It makes you think about survival.

It has the potential to agitate your feelings of belonging as well as your ability to learn and grow. People may feel threatened, and their reactions will be powerful and passionate. And so you want to be able to empathise with it and remember what it's like to be terrified or confused and anxious. You also want to be compassionate to others. You may still have to deliver bad news, but you don't want to come across as detached or uncaring since people want to be seen and heard. That is always the case. People require a sense of being seen and heard. In a crisis, though, they require it much more than usual. As a result, you want to be able to validate what you're hearing.

You want to demonstrate that you're paying attention and reacting to their concerns. However, you should do so with confidence and composure. So remember to use your emotional intelligence skills, listen, affirm, and reflect on a time when you felt similarly so you can connect with them truly from a place that counts. It's critical to have a strategic communication plan in place during a crisis. That you understand exactly what you're conveying and why you're conveying it. Then, because you'll be sending out regular updates, you'll want your communication strategy to be a reliable source of information for them to rely on.

Give them something to track so they know this is the most up-to-date information and that it takes precedence over the last time they heard from you. There are a variety of inventive ways to do this. However, you want your communication cadence to be constant and something people can rely on. It's therefore fine for you to change your mind about that strategy. As for what you know today, something new has been developed, and thus this is where you are now. When you link them together, it gives people a feeling of progress, and they can understand where you are on this trip, even if you can't tell them what the ultimate result will be like.

All leaders will have to improve their crisis management skills. The fact is that crises will become more prevalent in the future. The epidemic served as an example, but it will not be the last. They'll also be arriving more regularly. Other types of natural calamities, such as earthquakes and tsunamis, are also possible. There's geopolitical unrest, such as wars, and you're now so internationally connected that an issue in one area of the world will have a significant influence on people in all other parts of the world, including your employees, customers, and everything else. As a result, you'll want to get in the habit of having some crisis management abilities in your arsenal.

A few things to keep in mind are that when individuals are in a crisis, all of their survival mechanisms are activated. The amygdala is the portion of your brain that controls fight, flight, and freeze responses, as well as produces adrenaline and cortisol. It's a good thing, too, because it aids you in surviving a crisis. However, it is also extremely harmful to the body, and people are unable to maintain this condition for lengthy periods of time. People begin to feel burnout when a crisis lasts for a long period of time, and this includes both physical and emotional fatigue. What's intriguing is that your systems are intended to draw on that adrenaline and cortisol reserve for roughly an hour.

In an unclear situation, you must make decisions. And it is the most difficult task confronting leaders during and after a catastrophe. The element of emotion is one of the defining characteristics of a crisis. Emotions are usually quite strong. VUCA (volatility, uncertainty, complexity, and ambiguity) is an acronym that stands for volatility, uncertainty, complexity, and ambiguity. And it makes you uncomfortable when you are put into VUCA scenarios, such as a VUCA setting. As a result, you have what's known as a *"fight or flight"* reaction. You must project a sense of command. In this VUCA atmosphere, you've got to come up with a strategy, right? Consider that for a moment. It's dynamic, ambiguous, and complicated. It's a bit hazy, but it's starting to take shape.

One of the characteristics of a crisis is that nothing is certain about what will happen next. So, as a leader, how can you maintain control while your emotions are out of control? Right, you can see the writing on the wall, and you can see the consequences for your company, organization, and industry. And there's a lot of ambiguity and complexity. How can you get control of your emotions so that you can lead your business in a stable, consistent, and controlled manner?

You must prepare for the worst-case scenario. So you're dealing with a crisis before it ever becomes an issue. You're practising how you'd react in the case of a real-life disaster. It's referred to as muscle memory. You've practised it enough so when the crisis occurs, you already have the skeleton of a plan and you've previously rehearsed it enough that you can fall back on your muscle memory when the crisis occurs, not if it occurs. So, one of the first things you should do in a crisis is press the stop button, right? After you've regained control of your emotions, you may begin gathering information. In a crisis, there is no longer a scarcity of information. It appears to be the case.

So, how can you tell the difference between the wheat and the chaff? How can you be certain that the information you're receiving is accurate and relevant to your situation? They may be giving you useful information, but it has nothing to do with your business or sector. So, how can you know if a source is trustworthy or not? This is a difficult one, but what I encourage is that you look in the places you would ordinarily look, which is fantastic because you acquire knowledge, but it also plays into confirmation bias. In other words, you're hunting for evidence that already backs up your point of view.

It's critical to have as much knowledge as possible and to be aware of your prejudices, particularly confirmation bias. You all have blind spots, and when it comes to making key decisions as a leader, it's vital to obtain as much information as possible from a wide range of sources, even those who disagree with you. So acquire information in a crisis. That's fantastic, but what information do you have? Take a look at your organization. Take a look at what you're doing. What are the aspects of your business that are extremely critical to your success?

As a result, you will be forced to make judgments in a crisis. Some choices will now be made through a process known as triage. If the building is on fire, the decision is simple: everyone must exit the premises. Don't worry about the computers. Don't worry about anything; just get out; lives are on the line. Most of the time, your emergencies will not be as urgent, but you must keep this in mind. As a result, your choices will be prioritized. To keep your organization viable, to keep moving forward, to keep people safe, and so on, you'll need to make certain decisions first. Now that you're no longer in immediate danger, you'll need to make some decisions.

One of the things you've learnt in a crisis is that you have to make a decision based on the facts you have. That information might be altered the next day. You'll have to select a new choice now. It might be months or years from now. That isn't to say you made a poor judgement; rather, it indicates you made the best decision you could with the knowledge you had. So, one critique I've heard from many leaders is that it makes them appear wishy-washy. That makes you appear to be vacillating, as if you can't make up your mind. As a leader, your job is to make sure it doesn't appear that way, which means explaining your reasoning when you make a choice.

So, one of the characteristics of crises is that they are transient, correct? They will come to an end at some point. They'll ultimately go away. Some have a big finish, while others have a lengthy tail. However, things will inevitably fall apart. They will arrive at a new or next normal. And what do you do as a leader in those situations? What you'll do is reflect individually, then gather your team around you, including folks with diverse viewpoints and people who believe differently than you, and ask, "Okay, what did you learn throughout this?" "How should you proceed in the future?" "Is there anything you should never do again?" because it hadn't actually come to an end.

So, maintaining team motivation and spirits may be a genuine struggle for leaders amid a crisis. I believe that they, like many others, are seeking a leader to lead them through a crisis. At the same time, they're navigating their way through it like the rest of you. For leaders, the time when they must consider rotating their entire organization in a new direction can be extremely difficult. They must be extremely quick on their feet, and they must readjust and lead their team in a whole new direction. As a result, they must be able to exercise a great deal of imagination, which might be difficult at times.

An effective leader, on the other hand, moves through it and allows some creativity so that they may come up with new methods to lead their team. The most important thing for a leader in a crisis is to allow himself to be innovative. You're in the position of having to respond to people all of the time. And I believe it is critical that you give yourself the time and space to answer questions and find answers in a conscious manner. That may be as simple as pausing for five minutes before entering a team meeting to appreciate all of the obstacles that everyone is facing.

Perhaps putting the brakes on any and all forms of email. You've grown so accustomed to receiving emails and texts, as well as having information on social media, that taking a break from those modes of communication and reverting to more fundamental, one-on-one verbal conversation may be an effective method to communicate with your team. You often think about things from your perspective during a crisis, and when you're leading a team, it's critical to listen to what others are saying, how people are feeling, and even sometimes during a crisis, people can step up and actually communicate ideas that you never even considered, because you're still in your stressed brain.

And when you take a step back and listen to what people have to say, you can genuinely understand what they're saying and communicate with more compassionate language and more effective communication. You often believe that compassionate communication is exclusively concerned with how you can explain to someone what you want from them. But, in reality, stating that you want assistance, as well as indicating that you may require additional time, can be difficult. Can you meet the deadline they've set for you? And if you can't, how are you going to go about it? And being able to create a foundation, I believe, is critical during a crisis so that everyone is on the same page.

When everything is going well, everything is going well. You don't employ your backup plans. When things start to go wrong in times of crisis, it's important to activate your contingency plans. That's when you should start involving them and searching for more contingencies. You should ask yourself, "Where do you believe you're going?" But what are some of the potential pitfalls? Things are already going wrong in a crisis, and you don't have all the knowledge you need. As a result, it's critical that you investigate your options. What are the many scenarios that may occur? And consider this: what will you do if this occurs? What are your options if this occurs?

The more of that you can think of, the better you'll be able to react to it. Another thing you may do is inform your colleagues about the situation. These are the items over which you have control. This is the power, this is the type of domain of control, if these things happen. These are your decision-making degrees of freedom. These are the issues I'd like you to respond to. because you won't be able to reply to everything as a leader. As a result, you'll want to be able to use your team and give them some experience dealing with such possibilities. So, once again, every circumstance is different.

Teams, in particular, will look to you in times of crisis. But part of the problem is that they're going through the same things you're going through. All of the factors that are impacting you, such as loss of control and uncertainty about what will happen, are also affecting them. And you know that in order for teams, workers, and even individuals to function well, they need some semblance of self-efficacy, control, and autonomy. And, if you think about it, one of the things that crises tend to take away from you is autonomy, right?

That you don't feel like you have the autonomy to do or act, and that, organizationally, directives, *"This is what you're doing,"* and how you're going to respond to it, come down often. In times of crisis, it's crucial to realise that your teams still need those things, and perhaps even more so. So, finding methods to give them a say in your decisions, communicating with them, engaging them, and giving them that type of freedom of power, to say, *"These are the things that you get to make decisions on."*

It's difficult to express empathy for employees with whom you don't get along. However, you must find a way to exhibit some compassion in order to achieve commercial outcomes. Managing tough peers with empathy, compassion, and a desire to repair the relationship necessitates taking a step back in a method known as *"Step Back."* Let's have a look at it. Stop longing for a different outcome. Allow challenging coworkers to be themselves. It's best not to label them. Concentrate on the problem at hand rather than the individual. Better still, instead of attempting to change people, concentrate on improving the way you interact with them. Take control of the situation. It's never a smart idea to put off dealing with a tough coworker.

Assume responsibility for the relationship's improvement. Decide what you want to achieve, what behaviours to confront or ignore, and how to communicate. Not about the coworker, but too. Set aside your ego, as it may be the source of the problem. According to research, workplace conflict is primarily caused by feuding egos. Adjust your approach to avoid stomping on their ego while maintaining your own. Instead of scorn, go with curiosity. Don't allow yourself to be irritated by that coworker all of the time. Consider it a fascinating study of human behavior—a quest to discover why individuals behave the way they do. As difficult as it may be, get to know them and their position better. Keep the acronym going.

First, examine your reactions to stressful situations. Are you being your best self and exercising self-control, or are you responding out of proportion? Are you being objective and optimistic? Assumptions about its purpose must be abandoned. Instead of assuming a coworker's motives, try to figure out why they're acting the way they are. Difficult individuals almost never perceive themselves in that light. In most cases, they have completely reasonable motives for their conduct, such as insecurity or a lack of training. Small bridges should be built. Even modest gestures of compassion, empathy, validation, and forgiveness can help to improve relationships. Get rid of your defensiveness. Rather than arguing, use recognition as a default. To start, look for things you share in common. Keep in mind that you get to decide how much control you give them over you.

You may have to make the decision not to let a difficult coworker get you down, not just to exhibit empathy for yourself but also to keep part of your empathy for other coworkers. So take a step back to improve your connections and outcomes. Is there a more basic leadership role than creating goals? I don't believe so. Despite this, many leaders overlook the chance to design objectives based on empathy in a way that inspires people since it is something that they care about. As a result, it also influences outcomes. Begin by asking this question to develop relevant goals that demonstrate you're thinking about things from the employee's point of view. What is the benefit to them?

Efficiency Vs Effectiveness

Two essential levers for improving production are efficiency (is work done in a way that maximizes resources) and effectiveness (is work done in a way that maximizes output). Distinguishing between leadership and authority Many individuals confuse leadership with a job and equate it with power and influence. Leadership is better stated as a process or an activity. Others delegate power rather than leadership to you, and you are expected to provide your expertise, carry out certain tasks, generate ideas, or perform a service. Every position has a defined scope of authority that explains what is expected of you and what will satisfy those who have entrusted you with responsibilities.

If a district is to prosper, leaders must always offer coherence to the continuous improvement process by buffering it from—or tying it to—other imperatives in the district at any particular time. Without any buffering or bridging, teachers will be confronted with competing demands, making it difficult to generate anything coherent. For example, you investigated the development of a year-long constructivist biology course that forced students to engage in activities that needed a more conceptual, active approach to biology than is often required. Everyone bears the burden of leadership, and it is accepted by the one in the best position to make a decision or take action. The ability to share leadership is at the heart of adaptive leadership.

"The greatest leader is not necessarily the one who does the greatest things. He is the one that gets the people to do the greatest things." - Ronald Reagan

Business executives must accept and change at a much faster rate than ever before as a result of the rapid changes brought on by developing technology. Technological disruptions have become the norm in today's world, affecting almost every industry and area, from healthcare to manufacturing to computers. As a result, corporate culture must evolve to keep up with technology advancements and fast-changing client demands. As a result, in the twenty-first century, corporate leadership demands a proactive strategy to manage change and its influence on long-term organisational success. Communication, problem solving, interpersonal skills, human connections, teamwork, decisiveness, tenacity, and resilience are all cognitive soft talents and traits that modern leaders will require. Effective leadership is more important today than ever as digital technology is changing every aspect of how business is done. Leaders in the twenty-first century must constantly innovate and skillfully handle disturbances. In a continuously changing business climate, corporate leaders must be more flexible and resilient, focusing on creating and attaining tough goals, outperforming the competition, solving challenges decisively, and inspiring employees to perform at their best. Rapidly shifting customer expectations, induced disruption, increased market fragmentation, fast changes in economic development potential, and fluid labour markets are all characteristics that will make boardrooms very resilient.

Imagine a world where practically everyone is motivated to go to work when they get up. This isn't some far-fetched fantasy. Great leaders are establishing settings in which teams trust each other so much that they would lay their lives on the line for one another in many successful organisations. Regardless of the incentives given, other teams are condemned to infighting, disintegration, and failure. Why? Cynicism, paranoia, and self-interest are common in today's workplaces. The finest organisations, on the other hand, encourage trust and cooperation through fostering what the author refers to as *"collective collaboration."* It distinguishes the team's security from the difficulties outside. Everyone feels a sense of belonging, and all of their efforts are focused on defeating the common enemy and capturing significant chances.

Losing a game will be viewed as a learning experience, and the team will recover and prepare for the next game. They'll be able to empathize with people and put themselves in their shoes to understand what they're going through. Players are encouraged to take charge and make their own judgments.

Leadership necessitates cognitive abilities, which, as previously indicated, are increasingly important at higher levels of management. The ability to grasp how several components interact is part of cognitive complexity and systems thinking. Understanding how the many elements of the organisation interact with one another, how changes in one area of the system influence the other parts, and how changes in the external environment affect the organisation are all instances of this skill.

In the face of ambiguity, leadership is defined as someone who likes making decisions and is concerned about whether their judgements will result in desirable outcomes. How comfortable and joyful it is for a leader to make challenging unilateral decisions determines whether they are qualified for core, effective, or adaptive leadership. How many times have you heard a leader say, *"That's policy,"* without explaining where it is stated or what you may expect as a result of the policy? A staffer, in my opinion, is a leader who recognises a problem and responds with standard responses rather than seeking to solve the situation.

In both developed and emerging markets, where aged CEOs are leaving and new markets are failing to keep up with rapid expansion, leadership is in limited supply. Due to today's fast rate of change, command and control leadership has become outmoded.

Effective leaders plan ahead, set the tone, manage resources, encourage participation, hold people responsible, and generate results. There are no easy procedures in good times, let alone in uncertain times. Leadership begins at the summit of the pyramid, but it does not end there. High-performance companies employ three primary levers to create leaders at all levels.To demonstrate that people are capable of leading others, the capacity to be a leader must be gained and merited.

Why are some people and businesses more inventive, forward-thinking, and successful than others? And why do they seem to be able to replicate their success?

Master these paradigm-shattering paradoxes to become a next-generation leader with high emotional and social intelligence who can orchestrate great collaborative results. The author provides you with instances of people whose names you will remember, and what you will notice is their excitement for others. They've set out on a quest. They understand their objective and, even if they make mistakes along the way, they are able to learn from them. Rather than putting up with your boring life, imagine yourself in the shoes of a great leader and become one.

You can take a new leadership edition of Gallup's strengths finder programme with a unique access code. The latest edition of this programme includes specific tactics for leading with your strengths as well as the ability to plot your team's strengths using multiple domains of leadership strength disclosed in the book. This book highlights numerous steps to being a more effective leader based on compelling evidence: identifying your talents and investing in others' strengths; assembling a team with the correct skills; and comprehending and addressing the four fundamental requirements of those who look to you for leadership.

Gallup scientists have been reviewing decades of data on leadership while trying to learn more about strengths. They looked at over a million work teams, did over 20,000 in-depth interviews with leaders, and even spoke with over 10,000 followers all around the world to find out why they followed the most significant leader in their lives. For today's busy leaders, a new kind of leadership book that will encourage you to lead from the heart. It is written in an easy-to-digest inspirational style for leaders at any level of business, unlike other leadership books. The goal of this book is to help you improve your motivation and practise leading people at their best. This book is for you if you are a first-time leader or a top organizational leader in need of some insight or motivation. To lead with effect, you don't need a huge title or a business degree. What you need is practical wisdom: the insight, judgement, and character strength that all great leaders possess but that are rarely taught in business schools or corporate seminars.

Newer Approaches For Gen Z

Some professional groups have allowed their excitement about leadership philosophy to blind them to its practical applicability. Every year, instead of implementing what they teach, leaders choose fashionable new books and speakers, causing managers to become disorganized as they try to stay on top of best practises. The days of theory over practise are finished as Gen-Z joins the workforce in droves. Members of Gen-Z are realistic and focused, whereas Millennials were experience-driven and high-minded. They want regular face-to-face meetings with their bosses, plenty of telecommuting freedom, and opportunities to make a difference through their work. They witnessed what happened to Millennials during the late-2000s financial crisis.

Gen-Zers don't only want to avoid the same fate as their parents; they want to make sure that others don't have to. They aren't the only ones who want to see a change in leadership. Employees of all ages now have more context to appraise their bosses because to increased access to information. Managers, on the other hand, are out of excuses. In 2022, anybody in a leadership position should understand what workers expect and how to meet those expectations in ways that benefit both employees and the companies where they work.

As a result of market rivalry and the fragility of industrialized societies that rely greatly on the quality of goods and services, the subject of quality management has undergone quick and extreme development. The author presents top-level managers with the particular, field-tested procedures they need to effectively lead their organisations on the path to excellent quality in this companion volume. Managers have long recognized that becoming more competitive is the best reaction to a competitive situation. Quality improvement is perhaps the greatest source of competitive advantage for today's knowledgeable managers. They understand that quality improvement programmes offer some of the best returns on investment. However, the methods through which management may provide the leadership required to achieve quality are limited.

"Alone, you can do so little, you can do so much when you work together." -Helen Keller

During times of chaos, your leadership job portrays you as a great collaborator, bringing together brilliant brains, efficient methods, and unique viewpoints. By the reading of this book, you'll have a better understanding of how mentality, organisational culture, creativity, and sense-making all work together to provide you the tools you need to face the unknown. The first step in leading amid turmoil is to change your mentality. How your team approaches problem-solving is influenced by your conviction that your team will discover a solution to the problems you're experiencing.

Future IT leaders should be able to demonstrate knowledge and skills in a variety of fields. They require expertise in process engineering, software development, IT security, infrastructure architecture, data analysis, business intelligence, and other areas, in addition to the latest technology. At the same time, tech-savvy businesses must guarantee that technical executives demonstrate sufficient leadership, ownership, and decision-making skills in order to assist and manage the teams under their supervision. Overall, in 2022, tech leadership roles will be more spontaneous, multifaceted, and ROI-driven, with C-suite tech executives having heightened business acumen.You have a fantastic opportunity to collaborate thanks to your common experience.

Companies' needs alter as the market evolves. While leadership has always been a component of the culture of the firm, it is evolving. Excellent leaders should be able to guide a firm to success, assist their workers in being more productive, and establish a company-specific workplace culture. Companies should be aware of a number of leadership trends in order to stay competitive. With that in mind, you'll look at the several sorts of leadership statistics that every firm should be aware of in order to improve their business, leadership, and overall trajectory.

After obtaining little gratitude from their supervisors, a whopping 79% of employees will resign. 69% of Millennials are concerned that their employers will not allow them to grow as leaders.Only 15% of boards of directors are comprized of women. Developing leaders is crucial in business, according to 83% of firms. According to a Gallup poll, great managers have the following skills:

- They provide total transparency, in addition to building trust and open communication.
- Productivity, not politics, drives their decisions.
- They motivate and engage all of their employees through compelling goals and visions.
- They promote a culture of unambiguous accountability.
- They have the ability to influence results, overcome hardship, and overcome opposition.
- The accomplishment of long-term success is the primary aim of any company leader.

There are several leadership talents that must be cultivated in order to succeed.Leadership abilities are vital not just for starting a business but also for retaining and developing a staff. Leaders in their present firms rate the quality of leadership at 48%, up from 34% in 2011.

According to a recent poll, the top problem for 55% of CEOs is developing the next generation of leaders.

This makes sense, given that 63% of millennials say their companies aren't completely developing them as leaders in preparation for management jobs.Employee retention is plainly harmed as a result of this, since many people are not recognized as potential leaders fast enough and leave for other chances, as current employee recognition statistics demonstrate. In reality, just 11% of HR leaders believe they have a strong bench capable of filling leadership jobs when they become available, resulting in greater leadership shortages.

Almost 60% of leaders said they were exhausted at the end of each day, which might be a sign of burnout. According to a recent poll, 44% of executives who feel tired and used up want to relocate to a different organization to advance their careers. Within a year, 26% of the same respondents want to leave their current company. Approximately 44% of executives who felt exhausted at the end of the day planned to move their businesses in order to progress, with 26% planning to depart within the year. Those with outstanding leadership potential have been put under even more pressure.

According to a survey of over 1,000 high-potential workers, 86% of them were weary by the end of the day, an increase of 27% over the previous year. More than 77% of firms say leadership is missing, which is a large figure but not surprising considering the fact that 10,000 Baby Boomers retire every day. Simultaneously, 83% of businesses believe that developing leaders at all levels is critical. Despite this, just around 5% of businesses have adopted leadership development at all levels.

Why Women's Leadership Matters?

According to recent survey data, many businesses are experiencing a succession planning dilemma. The process of preparing people for leadership roles appears to be unproductive. Half of the respondents claimed their organizations needed enough leadership capacity, and 47% indicated there would be a future scarcity of leadership or executive-level capabilities. Women outperformed males in 17 of 19 criteria that distinguish exceptional leaders from ordinary or weak leaders, including creating connections, cooperating, and communicating.

"In the future, there will be no female leaders. There will just be leaders."

According to a Harvard 360 assessment from 2019. Women hold just 29% of top leadership positions in the world. At least one woman will have a senior management position in 87% of mid-sized businesses in the world. One issue has plagued schools, organizations, corporations, and people all across the world for the past 17 years: Where are the women in leadership? Not only in America, but all across the world.

"I feel really grateful to the people who encouraged me and helped me develop. Nobody can succeed on their own."-Sheryl Sandberg

When Arundhati Bhattacharya became the first woman to lead the State Bank of India, she created history (SBI). She had to overcome several obstacles before landing the sought-after position. Her memoir, *"Indomitable", a* working woman's notes on work, life, and leadership, chronicles some of them. Arundhati's life exemplifies the concept that hard work pays off. She would not have lasted long enough to head the SBI if she had handed away her power to insecure males at work. The four-year term of Arundhati Bhattacharya as CEO of SBI came to an end on October 6. Her term coincided with the banking sector's bad-loan troubles and the ensuing firefighting to put out the fire. She also laid the groundwork for SBI's affiliate banks to combine with the company, which was accomplished earlier this year. In 2016, Bhattacharya was included in Forbes' list of the World's 25 Most Powerful Women. Her winning slogan is that a person should be more action-oriented than thought-oriented. This makes it easier to deal with stress.

Half the fight is won for her when it comes to putting the right person in the right location. "Stress is thinking the worst," she adds,

"but if you're doing what has to be done, imagination takes a back seat."

She thinks that rather than being destructive, one should respond to faulty thinking in a constructive way. To refute an illogical argument, she believes that the other party must grasp your position. She believes that a leader must be patient, tactful, and goal-oriented. She continues to yearn for knowledge while holding one of the most prestigious positions in Indian finance. State Bank of India, or SBI, the India's largest bank, has undertaken a number of ground-breaking innovations that have become a pattern for public-sector banks, which control more than two-thirds of the country's banking industry in terms of deposits and advances. Consider the merger of five affiliate banks, a mammoth undertaking that went through without a hitch. With combined assets of Rs 40 lakh crore, the merger has elevated SBI to the top 50 banks in the world. The country's second and third largest banks have assets of Rs 7-8 lakh crore. While some opponents believe the bank is taking on too much, the merger's success or failure will be determined by the success or failure of the transaction.

Arundhati has, on the other hand, built a solid basis for the bank, allowing it to profit from economies of scale. A large-scale human resources revamp is one of the measures. She's implemented a *"perform or die"* mentality, implemented a new assessment system with budgets and objectives, and begun the process of developing specialized talents and leadership. These actions would go a long way toward assisting the bank in competing with private-sector competitors. She has also overseen the bank's digital transformation and used social media to communicate with consumers. According to sources, Bhattacharya is meticulous, competitive, and has good people skills as well as the capacity to take risks. Her extensive experience in corporate banking, retail, treasury, HR, investment banking, and a foreign assignment has also helped her.

Women are frequently overlooked for their leadership ability. They're caught in a dilemma, having to choose between being liked and respected, when neither is enough to get a place at the table. Organizations must evolve, but what can an ambitious female leader do in the meantime? It's not easy being a woman banker with a family in a position that is regularly transferred. There were times in Arundhati's life when she was on the verge of abandoning her job to balance her own goals with her family's requirements. She didn't give up, though. Instead, she approached her obstacles with a sense of humour and optimism, treating each project as a new chapter in her learning and adaptation process.

As chairperson of SBI, she guided the bank through some of its most trying times. When the NPA problems resulted in a huge public trust deficit, she encouraged confidence in the banking system. Under her leadership, SBI transformed into a customer-centric, digitally sophisticated bank under her leadership, while also playing a key role in national growth. Some of her human resources initiatives were industry firsts, which were well received and eventually emulated by other banks. Indomitable is a candid, honest, and humble narrative that will inspire you to take on new challenges, break down boundaries, push forward, and reach new heights.

In an interview with BT, she said, "I must have held a dozen jobs."

Many people believe that many issues remain unaddressed. The first is asset quality, with non-performing assets rising after the affiliate banks merged. Incentives, variable compensation, and employee stock ownership plans (ESOPs) will be critical to the HR overhaul's success in retaining and encouraging talent. A lot will also depend on the next chairman, who will be responsible for not just carrying out many of Bhattacharya's projects but also for establishing new ones. Leaders should focus on people's talents rather than their flaws while directing the game.

Arundhati advises, "One should place round pegs in round holes and square pegs in square holes."

She was able to shift the lowest-ranking branch to the second-highest simply by moving individuals around depending on their abilities, which increased production. A leader's short and long-term vision must be crystal clear. It may be difficult to build a long-term vision without enough data points, but the capacity to foresee and construct scenarios using those data points is critical. To achieve buy-in as a leader, you must communicate effectively.

"The easy days ahead of you will be easy. It is the hard days — the times that challenge you to your very core — that will determine who you are. You will be defined not just by what you achieve, but by how you survive.""Every woman I know, particularly the senior ones, has been called too aggressive at work. We know in gender blind studies that men are more aggressive in their offices than women. We know that. Yet we're busy telling all the women that they're too aggressive. That's the issue."

People are fascinated by Sandberg's leadership style because of her success and popularity. Knowing more about how she manages her staff at a firm like Facebook might be beneficial to others. Sheryl Sandberg, a transformational leader, praises her colleagues' accomplishments and thinks that praise motivates people to do greater jobs. Setting high expectations is also part of the style. Anyone who works under Sheryl Sandberg can expect to put their heart and soul into every endeavor. Those that fulfill or almost meet expectations are held up as models for the rest of the group. You might say that she is a laissez-faire leader to some extent because she is receptive to recommendations from others. Her staff are confident in approaching her with negative news because they know she will respond by helping them find solutions.

"We hold ourselves back in ways both big and small, by lacking self-confidence, by not raising our hands, and by pulling back when we should be leaning in."

Sandberg is often regarded as a transformative leader because she sets high goals for her employees, pushes them to achieve them, and rewards them for their efforts. She's a specialist at seeing a person's positive qualities and encouraging them to grow. She also understands how to motivate people to overcome personality flaws that prohibit them from progressing in life. When managers and employees work with Sandberg, they frequently learn that they are capable of far more than they previously realized.

"Just as our bodies have a physiological immune system, our brains have a psychological immune system — and there are steps you can take to help kick it into gear."

Sandberg's gentle prodding helps her coworkers become more successful, intelligent individuals who can focus on challenging tasks over time. In other words, she's the kind of leader that aids in the transformation of those around her. Sheryl Sandberg's leadership style consists of the following traits: Setting difficult goals; positive reinforcement is critical; appreciation for the effort that individuals make her learning agility allows her to swiftly become an expert in new areas.

"Bring your whole self to work. I don't believe we have a professional self Monday through Friday and a real self the rest of the time. It is all professional and it is all personal."

It is empathy that aids her in comprehending diverse viewpoints. She has self-awareness, which allows her to learn from her *"failures."* All of these traits contribute to her success as a transformative leader who knows how to stay focused on the big picture while also bringing out the best in others. Sheryl Sandberg has a transformative leadership style that pushes individuals to grow and become better versions of themselves. She recognizes that setbacks may teach people valuable lessons in both their professional and personal lives. She doesn't believe there is much of a distinction between these areas of life. She also pushes them to use what they've learned when faced with fresh obstacles.

"I realized that searching for a mentor has become the professional equivalent of waiting for Prince Charming. We all grew up on the fairy tale "Sleeping Beauty," which instructs young women that if they just wait for their prince to arrive, they will be kissed and whisked away on a white horse to live happily ever after. Now young women are told that if they can just find the right mentor, they will be pushed up the ladder and whisked away to the corner office to live happily ever after. Once again, we are teaching

women to be too dependent on others.”

Facebook is looking for leaders who can demonstrate empathy and enthusiasm. Sandberg excels at this, and her abilities boost everyone who works with her. According to her best-selling book, *"Lean In,"* the impostor syndrome may arise as a result of a lack of self-confidence, as per her best-selling book, *"Lean In."* It's also critical for women to start praising themselves for their accomplishments, no matter how minor. She made the contrast between men and women, saying that the former can list their abilities and traits, but their female counterparts are unable to accept what they are truly capable of.

“When you look at successful women, they have other women who have supported them, and they've gotten to where they are because of those women.”

Sandberg confessed in her book that every time she excelled at work, she felt that she had *"fooled everyone once again"* and that she would be discovered one day. Sandberg opted to share her thoughts when she first joined the social networking site in 2007. She requested that Mark Zuckerberg share his feedback with her once a week, and she stated that she welcomed criticism from his coworkers. Sheryl Sandberg decided to make Facebook a transparent organization within a month of arriving.

"Someone told her that the workers was unhappy because she opted not to utilize a PowerPoint presentation during her meeting with employees. That's when she realized that communication between a supervisor and an employee is critical, since misconceptions can lead to further difficulties and, as a result, have a negative impact on the firm."

Companies, like civilizations, come and go with the times. Some, on the other hand, last for generations, and the key is outstanding leadership. Great leaders may inspire people, help others see and believe in a goal, and drive the company's innovation. Everyone wants a strong leader at the top, including investors, consumers, and employees.

"Good leaders build products. Great leaders build cultures. Good leaders deliver results. Great leaders develop people. Good leaders have a vision. Great leaders have values. Good leaders are role models at work. Great leaders are role models in life."- Adam Grant

There are various characteristics that distinguish a successful business leader, including the ability to motivate people and the ability to articulate a clear vision that others can believe in. Excellent leadership is the only way to create long-term success.

"We cannot change what we are not aware of, and once we are aware, we cannot help but change."

It can only happen if you create an atmosphere in which everyone can look at your idea and say, *"Yes, this is where I need to be, or where I want to be."* People may regard you differently as a leader at various times. Still, in order to adapt to the situational management style, one must receive input and adjust; therefore, flexibility is essential. Second, even when you don't have enough data points, having a clear vision is critical. By communicating that vision and gaining buy-in, one may achieve the goals while using people's capabilities. Organizations are asking their leaders to stand up and guide the way ahead in a world of disruptive digital business models, augmented workforces, flattened organizations, and a continuing change to team-based work practices. CEOs are being pressed to take a stand on social issues; C-suite executives are being expected to collaborate more across functions; and line leaders must learn to work in networks of teams.

Leadership Trends

While organizations expect new leadership capabilities, my research shows that they are still largely promoting traditional models and mindsets—when they should be developing skills and measuring leadership in ways that help leaders navigate greater ambiguity, take charge of rapid change, and engage with external and internal stakeholders. I see leadership pipelines and development at a fork in the road, where companies must consider both the old and the new. Organizations recognize the need of developing leaders with long-term leadership abilities such as managing operations, supervising teams, making choices, prioritizing investments, and managing the bottom line. They also recognize the importance of developing leaders with the skills required to meet the demands of today's rapidly evolving, technology-driven business environment—skills like leading through ambiguity, managing increasing complexity, being tech-savvy, managing changing customer and talent demographics, and navigating national and cultural differences, to name a few.Many people clearly feel that companies require fresh leadership.

In this year's worldwide survey, 80% of respondents said they believe 21st-century leadership has unique and innovative criteria that are critical or extremely important to their organization's success. Included in the leadership manifesto a decade ago were topics like inclusivity, justice, social responsibility, recognizing the role of automation, and leading in a network. Many organizations are dissatisfied with their leadership programs as a result of these developments. Only 25% of respondents think they are successfully producing digital leaders, and only 30% say they are successfully developing leaders to tackle changing challenges.

A question is maintained and used to compute a general competence coefficient to the extent that it is effective in predicting whether a leader would have good or negative effects on their teams (to take the real assessment and find out your result, go here):

- *Do you have a special knack for leading others?*
- *Would the majority of people aspire to be like you?*
- *Do you make errors at work on a regular basis?*
- *Are you endowed with a charismatic personality?*
- *Do you believe you can do everything you set your mind to?*
- *Do you have a natural talent for office politics?*
- *Are you destined for greatness?*
- *Is it simpler for you to deceive others than for them to deceive you?*

- *Are you simply too gifted to pretend to be humble.*

"A leader should be visionary and have more foresight than an employee." - Jack Ma

Organizations are in a state of flux all of the time. Some initiatives are intended to bring about change, as in changes that are part of a strategic effort. Others occur as a result of a series of unanticipated events, such as an epidemic or natural disaster. Change may be tiring, regardless of the cause of it. In this book, you'll discover how to spot when your team is suffering from change fatigue and how to re-energize them. This is especially critical during chaotic times, when change occurs at a faster rate. Change management is more than a catchphrase. It's a constant reality for every company that wants to stay relevant.

"You must accept change as the norm, but not as your ruler," author Denis Waitley famously observed.

All of this change, however, comes at a cost to businesses in the form of staff change fatigue. Employees that are suffering from change weariness are less productive and engaged, which can be detrimental to the project's success. As a leader, you'll need to be able to spot when an employee is suffering from change fatigue and intervene as soon as possible. Look for clues in the form of physical, behavioural, or verbal cues. If any of the following is the case, they may be suffering from change weariness.

Is an employee, for example, looking more fatigued than usual? Or are they more irritated by the changes?

Is an employee who is typically outspoken now sharing less or acting unconcerned about a project's success?

Finally, this is where your ability to make sense will be tested. Take advantage of this chance to lead your team through the sense-making process with the purpose of better understanding your existing environment, what's feasible in that context, and how you can act to change it. Encourage your team to notice and learn from how their decisions affect the environment as you implement the concepts they've agreed on. Then urge them to be adaptable in the face of such changes. The fact that there is no one-size-fits-all answer can make turbulent times even more tough.

In general, easy answers are rarely used in leadership. Choose to adopt a more optimistic perspective today, one that prioritises the well-being of your team in your decision-making. Encourage a sense-making culture that values innovation and continuous learning. This will determine whether you are devoured by the turmoil that surrounds you or grow as a result of these leadership opportunities.

Power Points

- As a leader, you'll have to deal with a lot of challenges, hostility, and difficulties.
- Leaders couldn't wait for something unexpected to happen next. They have to constantly innovate and anticipate.
- During times of chaos, your leadership job portrays you as a great collaborator, bringing together brilliant brains, efficient methods, and unique viewpoints.

CHAPTER TWO

BUILDING CREDIBILITY

As A Leader Is Quite Challenging, But It Can Be Done.

"A real leader uses every issue, no matter how serious and sensitive, to ensure that at the end of the debate, we should emerge stronger and more united than ever before." - Nelson Mandela

You've probably heard the phrase *"credibility,"* but what exactly is it? It's the capacity to acquire real trust, integrity, and dependability—a characteristic that every leader in the workplace should possess. To develop credibility, you must be a trusted source of knowledge and decision-making among your team members. When it comes to displaying trustworthiness, however, actions speak louder than words. Others may lose faith in you if you don't follow through on commitments or make judgments that aren't strategically sound. It's not only for bosses to establish credibility. It will also be useful while you are seeking work in your field. Employers frequently want people who are skilled and ethical decision-makers, problem solvers, and communicators, in addition to being knowledgeable in their industry. Demonstrating your credibility by displaying proof of your successes and providing instances of team projects in which you have participated is an excellent way to do so.

"Being a good listener is absolutely critical to being a good leader; you have to listen to the people who are on the front line." - Richard Branson

What distinguishes a great leader from a competent leader is their ability to truly listen to, comprehend, and critically assess the various perspectives of their team members. Depending on the veracity of the comments, the leader may choose to accept, dismiss, or make suggestions to enhance the concept; but, regardless of the ultimate decision, the leader is truly interested in hearing what the team has to say and recognises the significance of varied perspectives. Compassion aids in bridging the gap between what the organization requires, what individuals desire, and what one is able to provide. And the most admired leaders are those that demonstrate compassion. According to a research, leaders that display forgiveness and compassion have the best success with their staff.

"There is no perfect fit when you're looking for the next big thing to do. You have to take opportunities and make an opportunity fit for you, rather than the other way around. The ability to learn is the most important quality a leader can have."-Anonymous

People want to work under leaders that inspire them while also providing stability and the capacity to shift direction when required. You must learn how to establish credibility, create the correct mindset for supporting and leading people, and cultivate innovative ideas that will benefit your company. When I think about credibility in the context of leadership, I consider whether or not you are someone that others want to follow. And I believe that the more of that person you are, the more effective a leader you will be. So I wouldn't suggest that establishing credibility is simple. It's one that necessitates consistency and visibility, so I wouldn't call it simple. But if you're fully committed to doing whatever it takes to earn that credibility, which means you'll show up and be visible, own your responsibilities and contributions, and put in the effort, I've found that it will become easier for you, and you'll start attracting opportunities for leadership rather than having to go out and seek them.

Whenever you're dealing with a long-term problem, remember to keep an eye on people's burnout levels and offer assistance. Another issue is that in times of crisis, individuals prefer to overwork rather than take care of themselves. So all of these things are interrelated, but if you're not cautious, you can have a work force that appears to be adjusting and performing well, only to have everyone tank and break apart. So, as a leader, you can help prevent burnout by taking care of your employees first and foremost.

Another thing to keep in mind is that when you start to notice indications of burnout, it will manifest itself in individuals being less productive, as well as increased stress and conflict. It will appear that individuals are becoming disconnected and sceptical. So, when you're delivering extremely difficult information during a crisis, and everyone's stress levels are already high, one or two things you can do is really come back to empathy. How do you think you'd want the information to be delivered to you? One thing is to communicate when it is acceptable. You often come up with solutions in the middle of the night, so I propose pausing and waiting until the morning meeting, or even getting up bright and early and scheduling that email to be sent at 8:00 AM.

So, how do you begin the discussion? by outlining the meeting's goal and expected outcome. Tell the other person why you're having the conversation and what you want to get out of it. I called this meeting, for example, to discuss a performance issue I'm witnessing. I'd like to tell you what I see, "get your understanding of the problem," and devise a strategy for *"changing the behaviour moving ahead."* Next, go right to the point of the conversation by sharing as much detail as possible about the facts you have. If you're dealing with a performance issue, for example, describe the behaviour you're seeing with specific instances and explain why it's a problem, then be specific about what you'd want to see instead and by when. To make it easier to absorb, provide good feedback first, then negative feedback, and then something positive again.

The paradigm may also be used to create objectives that are both sympathetic and encouraging. Set shared, demanding, compelling, and cooperative goals. As a result, everyone is working toward a common goal. It's tough enough that when it's completed, it feels really satisfying, and it's challenging enough that it pushes individuals out of their comfort zones so they may grow, but not so far that they feel overwhelmed. Set intriguing goals that will generate energy on their own and motivate individuals to go above and beyond. Meaningful enough so when individuals reflect on achieving the objective, it remains remembered and deserving of all their efforts. Finally, make goals that are collaborative in character.

Your capacity to influence and have an impression on others around you is critical to your professional success. You've all got pals or coworkers who always manage to score the greatest deals. It's not by chance, if you've ever wondered why. These people have honed their persuasive and engaging talents to the point that others are instinctively drawn to them. I will teach you how to discover and convey your skills, as well as how to use them to have a lasting influence at work, in this course. You'll acquire clarity on what makes you distinctive, how to leverage it to develop confidence, stand out forcefully online, and have more impact and influence with six critical skills suited for the modern workplace.FThe goal, or objective, might be to ensure that the individual understands the changes and to get their advice on future circumstances. Then, in a favourable manner, reframe the circumstances. Consider giving bad news to your team as an opportunity to give much-needed calm and counsel while also reinforcing your leadership persona. If you're giving negative feedback on a poor performance, use the meeting as an opportunity to show your support for your employee while also honing your management abilities. It may be difficult to recognise the benefits at first, but establish a habit of looking for and focusing on the good aspects before the meeting.

When someone has creative confidence, they believe in their capacity to use their imagination to come up with fresh ideas and have the courage to try them out. When a person is able to produce without nervousness or self-doubt, they are artistically confident. Why is it so vital to have creative confidence when it comes to cultivating a creative mindset? Creative confidence, in my opinion, is confirmation that a creative mentality exists and is actively operating. When individuals restore faith in their creative ability, they not only accept, but look forward to, the challenge of addressing more complicated issues with larger stakes and greater effect. They aren't only more prolific when it comes to generating ideas. They come up with superior ideas.

So, when you're talking about branding and leadership, I believe it's critical to think about it in terms of compartments. One is to consider what you want to be known for if you want your brand to stand out. As a leader, you must define how you want your brand's reputation to be linked to its consistency, awareness, and recognition. So one of these things is credibility. It is not only necessary, but definitely necessary for you to be a successful leader. You're attempting to build this funnel with your professional brand.

"As we look ahead to the next century, leaders will be those who empower others." - Bill Gates

If you make a promise to someone and then don't follow through, you will lose some credibility. With an explanation, you can lessen it a little, but you'll still lose some. You'll lose a lot of trust if you don't follow through on a major commitment or if you don't come through and don't explain why. And if you repeat this process numerous times, you will lose practically all credibility.

What leads leaders to make promises to their followers but then fail to follow through?

It's usually because they don't want to say no and want to please the person who requested it. That is why knowing when and how to say no is such a vital ability for leaders to master. If you want to maintain your credibility as a leader, which is one of your most significant assets, you have to be ready to have the difficult discussions now and say no, so that when you do say yes, you can truly go all out and make it happen.

Ask questions to ensure that you comprehend their point of view and that they understand what you're saying. Finally, get to the point of settlement. Obtain a consensual and thorough agreement on the future stages, including both parties' obligations. After that, make a written record of the conversation and keep the other person responsible for their stated objectives. To recap, while having a tough conversation, be clear about your goal and expected outcome, be direct and detailed, seek out the other person's perspective, and agree on future actions. Finally, keep in mind that practise makes perfect. The more you practise handling uncomfortable conversations, the simpler they get, and you spend less time and energy thinking about them. You'll eventually get rid of the term "challenge" from your vocabulary.

Then be sure to put that information to good use in order to enhance your project management. Pay more attention to how resources are allocated. Assign a fair timetable to team members who are suffering from weariness and provide them with the resources they need to succeed. Finally, teach the team stress management skills. Rest and recalibration, on the other hand, are required for you to properly handle change. Change fatigue indicators don't always allow you to relax, but you can assist your team and yourself by being aware of change fatigue indicators and understanding how to improve your team's change resilience.

Do you set deadlines that your team can't meet on a regular basis? Or do you set lofty targets that your team never achieves?

You'll soon lose credibility as a leader if this happens. This is frequently an indication of the same problem as a desire to please others. Someone may be pleased when you set a lofty goal for them, but they will be extremely dissatisfied if you fail to meet that objective. It's also possible that you're not very good at goal-setting or project management. In any case, you should (largely) achieve your objectives. You'll lose credibility if you don't. If you keep doing this, people will eventually cease taking you seriously, which is not a healthy position for a leader to be in. Leaders do not blindly support their followers. They do, however, continue to support their people, especially when they are in need. That is giving credit to others rather than claiming credit for yourself. It entails stepping in if one of your teammates has a problem with an unwilling partner. It entails standing up for your team members when they are subjected to unreasonable objectives or expectations from other teams.

It's never a bad idea to remind yourself of the wider picture and to put the worst-case situations out of your head. Finally, remember to take a deep breath. When you breathe deeply, you're sending a signal to your brain to relax and settle down. Your brain instructs your body to lower your blood pressure, calm your heart rate, and lower your stress hormone levels. You can return to a state of physical and mental peace by taking a few deep breaths. So keep in mind that planning is an important element of having a difficult talk. Define your goal and desired outcome, reframe the circumstances, avoid making predictions, keep things in perspective, and breathe.

"You need a commitment that is long-term and a commitment to leadership because that's the only way you build excellence." - Azim Premji

Nobody wants to fire someone, announce the cancellation of a project, or give a negative performance rating. However, as a leader, you must be willing to have unpleasant conversations. While you may not enjoy them, there are several best practises you can employ to keep the interaction peaceful, professional, and stress-free for both you and the other party. Allow me to guide you through the procedure. First and foremost, be ready to get right to the point when you begin the meeting; no waffling around, no chit-chat about the weather. People can usually detect when a conversation is going to be difficult, and any superfluous chit-chat only adds to their anxiety.

When you establish credibility in your industry among your coworkers, team members, and management, you gain opportunities to advance in your job. It's crucial to consider your effect on your workplace, whether you're just starting out or have worked your way up to a position of leadership.

Do your coworkers have faith in and respect for you?

Every industry undergoes changes. It's critical to have an ear on the ground for developing trends that affect the organization you work for, no matter how talented you are in your profession. This demonstrates to team members, managers, employers, and others in your sector that you are aware of current events in your industry and can adjust to them. If you withhold crucial information, your teammates and managers will perceive you as untrustworthy or dominating. That is why, even if the knowledge is bad, you should always be honest and share it with people. Embracing openness in the workplace is a terrific way to develop credibility.

"If you want to improve the organization, you have to improve yourself, and the organization gets pulled up with you." - Indra Nooyi

It's not simply that you want to have an effect and reach out to people; you also want to consider how it relates to what you want to achieve and the influence you want to have. Isn't it true that not everyone can be Elon Musk? Isn't it true that not everyone can be Mark Zuckerberg? However, you can make an impact in your own lane. So, when it comes to your professional brand, what do you want to be remembered for? What kind of influence do you hope to have? And what are the chances that people will seek you out for that? If you're known as a go-to expert in your field, they'll be more inclined to come.

So, for example, the Clifton Strengths Evaluation, the Personal Values Inventory, the Myers-Briggs, and the DiSC Assessment are some of the different assessment tools. When it comes to your professional brand, you have a top-down approach. You want people to identify your brand but also to be aware of it, so that whenever you show up, they know what you're renowned for, right? So you've mentioned Elon Musk before. Every time you hear his name, you know he's a strategic thinker, creative, and inventive.

According to research, one of the most important determinants of leadership effectiveness is bravery. Choose bravery as you consider what sort of co-leaders you want to be, the culture you want to co-create, and your commitment to bringing out the best in one another. When you're purposeful, have honest dialogues, and have strategic clarity about how you'll lead successfully side by side, you'll reap the rewards of co-leadership. Recognize the important conversations to have and decisions to make for a happy, healthy, productive, and pleasurable co-leadership experience.

If you're recognized as a go-to expert in your field, if you're credible, if you're consistent, and if you're visible, they're more likely to come. So, when you talk about trying to identify your own brand, I'm talking about myself as an individual or as a professional who aspires to be a leader or has influence. There are a variety of evaluations available to help you narrow down the things that are more consistent with your work style, right?

Credibility is earned by doing what you say you'll do and standing up for what's right. Leaders who accomplish this—and avoid these three frequent traps—are the most believable. Consider the following suggestions for increasing information transparency:

- Ascertain that each employee or team member understands their job duties, responsibilities, and tasks completely.
- Establish excellent communication channels so that employees are aware of where they may acquire accurate information.
- Be open and honest about your motivations and goals, and trust that the information you provide will be handled ethically and confidentially.

Three ways to display your brand so you can develop credibility It's crucial to consider your brand's consistency, exposure, and influence.

- *Is it possible for you to make an effect with your work?*
- *Are you a goal-oriented person? Are you a strategic thinker?*

- *Are you a creative thinker? Do you earn money for others?*
- *Do you find that as you work, you get more efficient, and as a result, the firm becomes more efficient?*

So, think about the effect of your work, and then think about credibility and all of that. I believe visibility is a marriage of the two, because the more visible you are, the more credible you become as a natural result, right? People begin to notice you and make the link, drawing a line and connecting the dots. So I believe that all of these factors are critical in helping to improve your brand in a consistent manner.

Staying connected and interacting with people is, in my opinion, the most important step for increasing your reputation. If you do all of the things you spoke about previously, such as communicate well, give off nonverbal indicators that suggest you're a leader, and plan strategically, but you don't connect with anyone, I don't think it will boost your credibility in any way.

So, as much as individuals tend to want to keep their leadership style task-oriented and tactical, I believe it's important to remember the human component of leadership. You must be able to communicate. That, I believe, has a lot to do with being able to adopt communication skills that are consistent with the message you're trying to convey and ensure that it reaches the people who need to hear it. So, when it comes to representing the sort of brand and leadership that you want people to respond to, communication is crucial. The behaviour is the last component. Is your conduct indicating to others that you're harnessing the presence of leadership only by studying your nonverbal cues? Last but not least, your mental processes are a vital aspect of embodying leadership.

Surround yourself with people who can inspire you to think beyond the box. For some of you, feeling and thinking a certain way for a long period becomes a way of life. Inquiring about perspectives from people outside of your settings and/or thoughts can assist you extend your viewpoint when it comes to efficiently using resources. Make an effort to create situations where everyone benefits. If there is a resource sharing agreement and you believe someone is intimidated by the idea of sharing, search for methods for all parties to feel accomplished. Last but not least, don't compare yourself to others. Concentrate solely on yourself, your individual or team goals. If you must compete, do so inside yourself. Strive for continuous progress in yourself or your team, and constantly keep learning in mind.

Don't be the person who grins and shakes hands at meetings but is uninterested in collaborating with others. While most individuals find being nice appealing, the effect is fleeting and will simply make it more difficult to create credibility. People who seem *"likeable"* yet aren't truly attentive to others are eventually seen as false or insincere.

Do you want to learn how to command respect as a leader?

One option is to provide constructive criticism and feedback. This demonstrates that you care about your team's performance and success, which will be beneficial in the long term. Consider the following suggestions:

- Even if the end wasn't perfect, share the results of tasks and projects.
- Presentations, newsletters, emails, and meetings may all be used to discuss performance data and make suggestions for changes.
- Praise team members' accomplishments in public and private and provide constructive comments.
- Seek out employee input, listen to others' problems, and be willing to try new ideas.
- Accept responsibility for your mistakes and show others how to recover from them. In your field, you can never have too much information and expertise. Continuing education and professional development courses may help you increase proficiency and industry knowledge, allowing you to become a reliable source of information.

And the more information you have, the more prepared you will be to lead. Consider the following possibilities if you want to advance professionally: Courses, workshops, and seminars for continuing education, learning new industry-related skills, and collaborating with other experts in your field. Don't only concentrate on your personal and professional growth. Encourage your coworkers and teammates to follow your lead. This will show that you care about the futures of your teammates. Here are some suggestions for promoting professional development:

- Hold regular meetings and provide suggestions for development.
- Share professional development resources with your staff on a regular basis.
- Establishing a peer mentorship programme is a good idea.
- Encourage your teammates to set objectives for themselves.

It's tempting for you as leaders to create an environment in which you are flawless. You have the ability to select companions, friends, and hire individuals who make you feel flawless at all times. You can always act as if you know everything.

The question is, how would you go about getting constructive feedback to help you grow?

Because a defensive mindset is by nature self-protective and self-deceptive, you'll find a lot of defensive habits inside businesses. Individuals or groups with a protective attitude only seek out knowledge that will protect them. When the truth is perceived as a danger, it can be suppressed. As a result, judgments may be based on assumptions that are incorrect. When people are subjected to such interpersonal situations, they feel compelled to close up in order to shield themselves from shame and danger. Individual and group performance suffers as a result of this type of conduct. A productive attitude, on the other hand, allows for rational thought. It serves as a natural foundation for making educated and truthful decisions. It actively searches for tested knowledge and delivers constructive data to assist others in achieving better outcomes through group brainstorming. This is especially true in companies that are focused on getting results.

So, the next time you're having trouble understanding someone's actions or feeling irritated about a result that was obtained or not attained, consider the following to shift into a more productive mentality. You will develop knowledge and the capacity to alter them for new actions that convey a different message. Then try to be awestruck. Rather than leaping to conclusions, attempt to pique your interest in why and how something is happening and actively pursue inquiry by asking open-ended questions. Engaging in conflict is really beneficial to achieving shared goals.

Good leadership requires the ability to make informed and strategic decisions. Doing so on the spur of the moment might undermine your credibility and cause people to lose faith in you. Whether you're making large-scale judgments or smaller day-to-day decisions, they should always be well-informed. Try these basic strategies to improve your decision-making abilities and establish credibility: Consider what you want to happen as a result of your decision.In comparable scenarios, draw on your own decision-making experiences. Consider the advantages and disadvantages of your choice. Collect comments from your coworkers. Examine the result of your decision. Learn from your blunders if the outcome wasn't what you had hoped for.

Others may regard you as dominating and self-serving if you're the only one making decisions at work. Inclusion is essential for establishing credibility since it demonstrates your willingness to give your team members a seat at the table. When individuals work together, more good results may be obtained, and decision-making can be improved. Try the following ways to encourage collaboration:

- Participate in group projects and problem-solving activities.
- Allow members of your team to collaborate with you and share their thoughts.
- Create a work atmosphere that is devoid of judgement.

- Encourage openness and transparency.

Have you ever worked in an environment where you felt at ease or in a close circle of trust?
Do you know what piqued your interest?

These micro-moments determine your experiences at work and in life in general. These are isolated moments of connection that you have in a certain setting. They can be expressed through eye contact, a smile, or simply being there. You discovered one feeling that was widespread in these micro-moments when examining high-performing firms. It is one's sense of responsibility. This refers to how much love and compassion individuals have for one another and how much they exhibit it.

There are several advantages to maintaining a caring attitude at work. I found that when employees have a caring mentality, they had fewer absenteeism, less burnout, better collaboration, and higher job satisfaction. Companies like PepsiCo, Southwest Airlines, and Google have begun to explicitly integrate caring in their leadership principles due to its quantitative worth. Control is the polar opposite of compassion. This is the degree to which a certain environment is seen to be regulated. These settings are mostly made up of conscious and unconscious policies and processes, according to us. What are the differences in dynamics between caring and controlling mindsets?

In many cases, you can avoid conflict situations. However, if you can sort of separate the goals for an impact from the conversation, it becomes a lot more doable. Finally, think about how you praise others. Instead of focusing just on the end, try to concentrate on the process, effort, and decisions. You know that research demonstrates that people who are praised for their efforts always surpass their prior level of achievement. Problems, critical comments, and recessions are all excellent learning opportunities. Remember, in the twenty-first century, all of you must become lifelong learners. While it may be uncomfortable at times, I strongly advise you to step outside of your comfort zone and allow yourself to be displaced from time to time.

Acknowledgement is essential for getting the most creative work from your team members. Acknowledgement entails not just seeing and verifying the reality of action and activity, but also expressing gratitude for it. To take it a step further, gratitude is more than just acknowledgment. Appreciation entails the adding of value as well. Individuals become highly engaged, creative, and productive when leaders acknowledge and promote the qualities and efforts of the people in their business.

"Integrity is the most valuable and respected quality of leadership. Always keep your word." - Brian Tracy.

Try implementing these recognition expressions into your contacts with your team members to let them know that they are being seen and that their efforts are appreciated. To begin, compose a celebratory letter or email. Two, just say *"good work" or "well done"* when giving favourable remarks. In person, especially during the time of their efforts, because it is when individuals are most in need of this validation. Three, they openly congratulated others on their efforts or a job well done. Finally, invite individuals in for a one-on-one conversation to raise their spirits. Make sure you look at your team members, their talents, and their job through the lens of opportunity to foster the growth of their creativity.

They broaden their possibilities by being willing to try new things, and they make better selections as a result. Furthermore, individuals who believe in their creative potential are not afraid to use their imaginations to imagine a better future and then apply their abilities to improve on current ideas in order to have a beneficial effect on the world. You have the honourable position of both leading by example and establishing an environment that supports and nurtures your creative confidence as a leader. By developing and displaying your own creative confidence, you offer people permission to explore, accept, and express their creativity. You'll also establish social proof, or the notion that this is how things should be done, by implementing practises and systems that support creativity.

The modern workplace is preoccupied with outcomes, with sales figures, product ROI, and profit margins. None of these things, however, would be achievable without work. Furthermore, most people are their own worst judges, believing that they are performing worse than they actually are. Low-level stress stifles the flow of innovative ideas, decreasing productivity, performance, and motivation. Stress is replaced with increased emotions and boosted morale on an individual and collective level when work well done is recognized on a regular basis. Recognizing effort boosts motivation and drives more than a pay raise; it feeds individuals regardless of whether they measure the efficacy of their job using internal or external metrics.

Thus recognizing work provides long-term advantages. They will help your personnel grow in confidence, allowing them to better deal with future obstacles. They will be able to realise their full potential as a result of their self-assurance and confidence. laying the groundwork for further chances later in their careers. Expand your perspective to truly appreciate your team's efforts, especially those that include and express innovative thinking and problem solving. Strengthen your appreciation practise with this unique dosage. Take a quick recognition audit and try to recall the last time you wrote someone on your team a note or an email congratulating them on a job well done, publicly recognized their effort, or just complimented their work in the moment.

Leadership is difficult, and all leaders make mistakes. It may sound absurd, yet it is true. Even Steve Jobs committed some huge blunders. You all demonstrate that you're human, that you're not always sure what you're doing, and that you don't have all the answers every now and then. You must acquire the trust of your followers in order to make your ideals a reality. Because you rely on people to get you forward, it's critical to detect the actions that can disengage and alienate your supporters.

Leadership is a collaborative endeavour. Employees who join your company and support your vision provide expertise and talents that can help you advance your plan. It's tough to relinquish control when you're aware that others may not act in the same way you do. Authentic leaders stick to their convictions. Genuine leaders, according to Harvard Business School professor and authentic leadership specialist Bill George, stay committed to their beliefs and objectives even when things get tough. They don't give up just because it's convenient to do so. Because they work from a position of complete honesty, they can be expected to show up the same way every time. Employees can tell when their bosses are faking it. Leaders must be cautious about the carrots they dangle in front of their personnel to inspire them. Employees have every right to anticipate that if a leader makes a promise, he or she will keep it. So many times, leaders communicate ideas in the heat of the moment, unaware that their staff are listening intently. When executives make recommendations or ideas, employees interpret them as demands or promises, according to Marshall Goldsmith's book, "*What Got You Here Won't Get You There*". Employees' confidence will be violated if you fail to deliver on a promise, no matter how big or minor.

"My job is not to be easy on people. My job is to take these great people we have and to push them and make them even better."- Steve Jobs

When you have a controlled attitude, you prefer to avoid emotions. Your stress chemicals are activated, making you scared and resistant to change. Sadly, this state can occasionally present itself in acts of emotional abuse and dominance. However, there is frequently a model of value-based beneficial actions in a caring attitude. As a result, positive neurotransmitters are released in your brain, increasing your ability to receive and give emotional connections. As a result, your mind becomes more open and you can better engage with your environment.

So, as a leader, how do you go from a controlling attitude to a caring one?

First and foremost, you must recognize that how you present yourselves as employees or leaders is heavily influenced by your surroundings. It's critical to establish work environments that stimulate collective cerebral ability, but you also need to consider how you support people's social, emotional, and psychological needs. Then you must demonstrate presence. You all have a desire to be seen, heard, and cared for, whether you are high flyers or suffering employees, janitors or Chief People Officer. Being present with your coworkers is your first obligation. Last but not least, remember to rejoice in times of connection. A brief celebration of a little partnership can help to validate one's self-worth while also fostering a sense of belonging among many people inside the business. Just keep in mind that caring for the sake of caring is ineffective. In any given relationship, one can never fake their way out of honesty.

Your staff are your most useful source of information about what's going on in your company. To overcome failures and adversity, leaders need thick skin. They also require a high level of self-assurance due to the sceptics who doubt their talents and would enjoy seeing them fail. Leaders, on the other hand, must check their egos at the door and guarantee that their personal goals are subjugated to the larger benefit of the firm. This might be one of the most difficult habits to break since it necessitates a high level of self-awareness and candour regarding personal motivation. Anger that is out of control has no place in leadership. Fear, disdain, a lack of control, and a lack of compassion for people on the receiving end are all conveyed. True, the stresses that come with being a leader are numerous and potentially devastating. Your workers, on the other hand, are not responsible for providing emotional support, which is why it's critical to seek out healthy choices and networks of support to express or discuss your emotions.

Leaders must avoid reacting emotionally, behaving defensively, not listening with an open mind, and blaming. Even if you are the brightest person on the planet, people will tyre of you and lose faith in you if you do not inspire them with productive activities. Increase your awareness and emotional intelligence by leading by example. One of the most common errors leaders make is failing to see that they are not just expressing their thoughts or opinions.

They are speaking on behalf of everyone who has chosen to follow them or join their group. That's part of the responsibility of being a leader.

At some point throughout their leadership, every leader will undoubtedly exhibit one or more of these traits. You are all human, after all, and leadership is difficult.Self-awareness is the most critical part of leadership development. You will be more effective at detecting and changing these detrimental patterns if youy are more self-aware, so that you may build your best companies and live your best lives. A leader's job is to ensure that their division or department succeeds. Naturally, the leader's credibility influences whether or not the people he or she leads trust and depend on them. Leaders in most business systems are defined by their credibility.

When it comes to delivering guidance to employees, precision is required. Ambiguity can indicate two things:

1) A lack of direction, and

2) Concealment.

Both of these impressions instil suspicion and distrust. The more clear your goal and direction are, the easier it will be to involve people. Information flowed from the top down through a carefully regulated funnel in conventional hierarchical companies. Employees just did their duties and received the exact information that management desired. Employees now have a strong voice. They are enabled to share ideas and observations in healthy cultures. Employees make important suggestions and want to be heard.

However, in a developing business, one individual—or even a team of leaders—can not perform all duties. Delegation that works allows you to stay focused on what you do best and what you like. Delegation not only increases your capacity to get things done and provides redundancy inside your company, but it also communicates your faith in your colleagues. Employees want to know that they are making a difference. They want to feel useful and capable. Employees have significantly different perceptions of their bosses and the C-level community than they have of themselves. Even if the leaders do not aim to divide the firm, there is a line of demarcation between leadership and the rest of the organization. It's all too easy for you to lose touch with your employees as your companies develop.

When it comes to developing appreciation tactics, you must be deliberate. It takes the entire system to keep the firm running well, and you must continually re-hire your employees to keep everyone motivated via gratitude and recognition. Favoritism is one of the most depressing leadership attitudes. While every business has inchpins who are critical to its success, companies should strive to be process-centric rather than hero-centric.

When a company is built on a small group of heroes, the remaining employees may begin to feel expendable. To reduce reliance on heroes, businesses must invest in the development of mechanisms that ensure that operations are not disrupted if important personnel depart. The department and the organization will grow if they are accountable to the individuals they are in charge of and work in their best interests. Unfortunately, it can be difficult to maintain credibility as a leader. Sometimes the leader does something that casts doubt on his or her own trustworthiness. In a lot of situations, it's nothing out of the ordinary.

Speaking or acting without thinking about, researching, or comprehending the topic, situation, or the audience is a typical mistake made by leaders that may be harmful. Leaders have the difficult responsibility of making judgments under duress and frequently in unusual situations. Leaders must use the time gap between stimuli and reaction, however long or short, to discover and analyse as many variables as possible in order to take the smartest and most informed decision.

Leaders that instil a scarcity mentality in their organizations pay a steep price. When resources are thought to be restricted, such as compensation, opportunity, or recognition, paranoia, fear, and politics grow. People feel fearful of making a mistake and concerned about their future. As a result, collaboration and creativity are harmed. A different focus is abundance. The term *"abundance"* refers to a large amount of anything. An affluent attitude boosts your confidence because you believe there is plenty in the world and that you can spend what you have on the things that matter most. Organizations that adopt this attitude become more lucrative, not because they concentrate on competition but because they concentrate on opportunity and synergy development.

Leaders with an abundant attitude widen their perspective to consider demands, timelines, and experience when allocating resources. Employees get the space and resources they need to connect to their mission, think creatively, and manage stakeholder relationships in exchange. To put it another way, people in such situations are free of future fear. As a consequence, people are better able to coordinate ambitions and collaborate on action, resulting in more meaningful development.

So, how can you make the mental transition from scarcity to abundance?

First and foremost, concentrate on what you have. If you feel drained or limited in your resources, make a list of everything available to you and others in your surroundings. The consequences are severe when leaders' deeds do not match their words. If a leader claims to respect openness but isn't transparent in return, they're really saying, *"Do what I say, not what I do."* Others are observing you as a leader, and it's crucial to realise that they are turning to you for direction and indications. They will be united with you if you are. The two aspects that leaders must maintain at all times are consistency and openness. The leader must speak honestly with the team to build trust. Furthermore, fairness necessitates uniformity among individuals.

Anything beginning with *"I," "me," or "mine"* should be kept to a bare minimum. Leadership is about the team—*"we"*—for effective leaders. When you put your attention on the team and utilise influence rather than authority to help them grow, your reputation rises. The degree of influence and trust that a leader has is directly proportional to their credibility. Leaders that wax lyrical or use meaningless language may find it difficult to gain respect. *"Be on point, be brief, and be seated."* That was the finest leadership instruction I ever heard. Leaders who accept responsibility for their errors and embrace them foster a culture of learning and growth rather than blame.

Leaders that are fearless of being wrong or making errors are essential for a healthy and successful organization. People will cover up mistakes rather than learn to drive the business ahead if the culture of an organization is such that no one wants to be incorrect. The most effective leaders value the time and intelligence of the people they lead.

Richard Branson's leadership philosophy is to "Say what you mean, mean what you say, and preferably in as few words as possible."

Leaders that place too much emphasis on *"command and control"* rather than *"collaboration and inspiration"* will have their reputations tarnished. Leaders that really endeavour to understand their workers' needs and motivations while creating the environment for them to flourish will be able to recruit and retain talent. The credibility of a corporation is built on its leadership style and culture. Leaders have a proclivity towards over-satisfying their customers. When a company does this, it usually ends up with low-quality products and promises that aren't kept. This leads to overpromising and missing deadlines, as well as going too hastily and sacrificing quality. Leaders must concentrate on the truth and recognise that customers prefer it. Customers, at the end of the day, desire quality and honesty.

It bridges a gap in the leadership application process by merging core leadership ideas and approaches with Life Lessons. Many of the leadership issues that you see today may be addressed using these life lessons. Many leaders *"fail"* due to a lack of wisdom rather than a lack of competence, experience, or knowledge. This book is a valuable resource that provides new ideas, insights, and inspiration that will undoubtedly alter your business.

Furthermore, by establishing practises and structures that support creativity, you'll establish the social evidence, or the idea that this is how things are done, that will affectively develop a creative culture within your firm. According to social contagion theory, each individual has an effect on people three degrees away from them, and pleasant sentiments spread quicker via social networks than negative ones. There is the potential for that good shift to ripple out to hundreds, if not thousands, of individuals, and to influence not just the culture of your whole firm, but the world beyond, by enhancing the creative confidence of your team members.

Being a self-sufficient superman is not a prerequisite for leadership. The traditional view of leadership is that it is exercised by a single individual. However, the finest leaders understand that excellent leadership is a team effort. Whether you're co-leading a project, a team, or an organization, whether you're leading in person, virtually, or in a hybrid way, whether you chose your co-leader or co-leadership happened to you, how successful you are as co-leaders will largely depend on how deliberate you both are about your leadership.

Having a personal social media account is a frequent way for leaders to undermine their credibility. You are your brand once you become a leader and visionary, and it must be displayed at all times, including personally. Cheating for short-term gain, no matter how cleverly concealed, will ultimately come to light, damaging both the leader's and the company's reputation. Things like compromising consumers' data while professing not to have done so have recently come to light from large corporations, jeopardising people's faith in their leaders. You will win the long game if you are straightforward and loyal to your statements. It may sound counterintuitive, but the largest mistake CEOs and executives can make is not chasing exposure.

If you're not speaking to the press or attending conferences, how can you be considered a thought leader?

If clients have never heard of you, how will they recognise your name? It's not going to happen. If they want to have an influence on credibility, all leaders must constantly promote their brand to the public. Leaders must lead, whether your organization is going through a corporate change or a big catastrophe. You may not see the shift approaching and hence be unprepared. When a crisis strikes, though, it's time to rally your team and do everything you can to assist the people around you in making difficult and critical decisions. What measures do leaders take during a crisis to refocus their efforts, develop a winning attitude, establish clear communication, and step up? How can you become a more adaptable leader, team, and organization during a crisis? Many leaders fail to assist one another during times of uncertainty. It's simple to point fingers and compete for position, so you must identify and reject this urge. Support your subordinates, peers, and other leaders who require aid and advice. It's vital not to become engrossed in your work. You must maintain an external perspective in order to anticipate and pivot rapidly when necessary.

"Innovation distinguishes between a leader and a follower." - Steve Jobs

Many leaders fail to assist one another during times of uncertainty. It's simple to point fingers and compete for position, so you must identify and reject this urge. Support your subordinates, peers, and other leaders who require aid and advice. It's vital not to become engrossed in your work. You must maintain an external perspective in order to anticipate and pivot rapidly when necessary. Leaders who can perceive and grab opportunities as they present themselves are especially important during difficult times. Leadership talents are not often associated with a title, but rather with forward-thinking individuals who are eager to stand up to the plate and buy into a progressive culture.

Leaders should be able to read people because nonverbal communication is frequently more significant than spoken communication. To stand out, leaders must pay attention to facial expressions, body language, and voice tone in order to understand what is truly going on with their employees. To put it another way, they should be socially conscious.

Leaders that excel are aware of why they are in charge. They put the cause first, and subsequently the organization. Great leaders anticipate, while good leaders concentrate on the present. Leaders such as Bill Gates and Warren Buffet are noted for their outstanding ability to predict future trends in their organizations or other industries in which they invest. To shine as a great leader, they must remain watchful at all times.

To shine as a great leader, they must be continually aware of future possibilities, opportunities, and dangers for themselves, their colleagues, and their company, in order to make the best judgments possible that will take them along the correct road. Great leaders overcome pomposity and gain humility by shifting their mindset to one of service to others rather than wielding power. This, in turn, inspires and elicits affection and support from their followers, resulting in improved team performance. Many times, good leaders say more than their subordinates. While a competent leader listens to their team members, they may not be actually listening; that is, interacting with and absorbing the unique thoughts and recommendations of others.

True leaders give credit where credit is due. It takes a strong, self-assured individual to admit they are mistaken. Another method is to praise individuals frequently and publicly when they perform good work or accomplish a job effectively.The finest leaders provide the advantage of the doubt by being fair and generous and providing a second opportunity or the benefit of the doubt to those who deserve it. Leaders that micromanage their teams prevent talent from flourishing, the talented from producing, and the experienced from maximising their abilities. Step aside and give individuals the space they need to achieve their best if you want to be a great leader. Even if business is serious, the finest leaders know how to create excitement and joy. If accountability and responsibility are important, don't allow slackers get away with it. When a competent leader follows through on his or her ideals and the team remains highly functional, he or she earns respect. When one trusts, it sends forth a signal.

When one trusts, it sends a message that one believes in and trusts others, which only encourages others to reciprocate! All is conquered by love. One is obligated to find the secret of leadership through loving the people, the organization, and those who are served.It's possible that the most critical abilities for succeeding as a leader aren't what you assume. Although being visionary and strategic thinker is crucial, a new study reveals that it is more anchored in daily interactions with people. A leader who has mastered good discussions is more likely to manage their team or organization successfully. Leaders who are likeable communicate on a highly personal and emotional level. They never lose sight of the fact that they're dealing with a real person. Likable leaders always have a positive attitude, which is evident in how they express things. Even in clearly terrible conditions, appealing leaders exude a positive outlook for the future, a belief that they can contribute to making tomorrow better than today.

When it comes to their successes and mistakes, successful leaders are calm and collected. They normally enjoy achievement without getting carried away with it, and they readily accept defeat without being irritated. They take what they've learned from both and go on. If leaders want to stand out, they need to constantly learn, assess, and be open to change. They should accept change as a necessary part of growth and value constructive criticism. They must examine themselves, their organization, and the processes in place as life-long learners in order to find better ways of being and doing things. No title or position will ever turn someone into the leader they desire if they lack the necessary leadership abilities. There is only one way to improve as a leader: to concentrate on their leadership abilities while also honing their competence in their industry. To stand out, a leader must lead by example; their deeds, rather than their words, should pave the way for others to follow. Mahatma Gandhi inspired millions of Indians to be self-sufficient by weaving khadi cloth on his spinning wheel and pushing the people to do the same. Great leaders provide an example for others to follow.

"A person who is happy is not because everything is right in his life, He is happy because his attitude towards everything in his life is right." - Sundar Pichai

A leader's ability to think differently can set him or her apart from the pack. Great leaders don't simply listen to and improvise on the crowd's ideas; they come up with totally new methods of doing things. Henry Ford would have ended up with nothing more than a faster-driven horse carriage if he had listened to his clients. Instead, he devised a more efficient horseless mode of transportation in the form of Ford automobiles! By observing and listening, one may have a better understanding of what is going on around them. A successful leader is usually an excellent communicator, both as a speaker and as a listener. Likable leaders honestly feel that everyone is worth their time and attention, regardless of status or skill. They make everyone around them feel good. Leaders should not only speak but also behave in order to generate trust and appreciation. Many leaders claim that integrity is vital to them, but it is much more crucial for them to demonstrate it on a daily basis. Even though a leader exudes appeal, if that charm isn't backed up by a firm foundation of honesty, he or she will be unlikable.

Leaders that stand out have integrity, which translates to dependability and trustworthiness. They are dependable because they are truthful. Because transparency begets integrity, the mechanisms that work under a great leader are transparent and hence trustworthy. Great leaders exercise honesty, even if it takes longer and is more difficult. While excellent leaders may appear honest and strive for the shortest method to get things done, great leaders truly practise honesty. Knowing how to connect with the proper people—those who can drive a vision ahead and build effective tactics—is an important part of outstanding leadership. To stand out, leaders should accept full responsibility for failure and allow their team members to shine when things go well. At a national news conference, Professor Satish Dhawan, the Chairman of ISRO, took full responsibility for the SLV-3 satellite launch failure at a national news conference instead of blaming his team for the humiliating failure. Leaders who want to stand out must be able to handle success and, more significantly, failure. Great leaders like leading not because of the enormous power it affords, but because of the significant responsibilities it entails. Great leaders seek more accountability and, as a result, focus on addressing their responsibilities with their best efforts. Good leaders focus on securing maximum power and holding onto it, whereas great leaders seek more accountability and, as a result, focus on addressing their responsibilities with their best efforts. This allows them to achieve the best possible outcomes for their organization while also allowing them to tap into their full potential.

Great leaders are sincerely concerned about the company and the cause for which they work. They don't squander their time planning to increase their authority. This aids in propelling their companies to new heights of accomplishment. When you can rapidly assess a person's abilities and strengths, you'll be in the greatest position to assist them develop and flourish in the most effective way possible. Charisma is more about getting people to like themselves while you're around than it is about getting people to like themselves when you're around. Good leaders should not only recognise the best in their employees, but also ensure that they see it in themselves. They should bring out people's abilities so that everyone improves themselves and the task they're doing. Outshining as a leader is not a given; it is earned through the development of transferable talents that are critical to one's professional success. Implementing the aforementioned methods will undoubtedly result in one's outshining as a leader.

Who is your role model, and why do you look up to him or her?

"Leadership is lifting a person's vision to high sights, the raising of a person's performance to a higher standard, the building of a personality beyond its normal limitations." - Peter F. Drucker

Tim Cook is the CEO of Apple, the world's most valuable firm. After Apple's founder, Steve Jobs, died of cancer in 2011, he took over the corporation. Cook has assisted Apple in navigating the post-Jobs transition as well as developing new product lines and building Apple retail outlets in China. All eyes were on Apple CEO Tim Cook as he took over from the iconic and brilliant Steve Jobs. People questioned whether he had the essential leadership characteristics to enable Apple to maintain its position as a technological powerhouse. People immediately realized that this is not the case, and that Tim Cook is more than capable of leading Apple to new heights.

"A good leader inspires people to have confidence in the leader. A great leader inspires people to have confidence in themselves." - Eleanor Roosevelt

Leadership necessitates the development of abilities that must be refined as your career progresses. A leader's life is not an easy one. Leaders are often forced to make extraordinarily tough decisions that have far-reaching consequences for the people around them. You must be able to trust in your capacity to take chances, even if they are challenging. Tim Cook realizes that in order to succeed, he must take chances.

"We take chances knowing that risks may occasionally end in failure, but there is no potential for success without the possibility of failure," Cook says.

It will be very hard to gain the complete support of those around you if you lack the courage to take measured risks. Tim Cook is significantly calmer and more restrained than Steve Jobs, who was always a flamboyant and unusual guy. This might be because he's concentrated and paying attention to what's going on around him. You should focus and jot down the crucial information as soon as you detect your thoughts drifting away from the conversation.

According to the traditional proverb, you have two ears and one mouth, so utilize them in that proportion.

Tim Cook is regarded as being a leader who values the input and opinions of the people he surrounds himself with. Understanding that you don't know everything is an important part of being a leader, and delegating some of the work to others on your team will go a long way toward helping you be a great leader. Apple is a firm at the vanguard of innovation, which necessitates a diverse group of people to help shape the future. Tim Cook recognizes that, as the CEO of a firm built on innovation, he requires thinkers who can provide fresh perspectives.

In a recent interview with Businessweek, Cook stated, "We encourage a variety of thinking." "We want a wide range of styles." "We want individuals to be themselves."

Many leaders lack the ability to bring out the best in others, and improving on this talent will give people the confidence to follow your example. Never lose sight of your origins. Tim Cook finds time to visit his Apple stores and interact with his customers, whether it's in person or by email. It's easy to get carried away when you're the CEO of the world's largest corporation. It's therefore critical to stay grounded.

"Not allowing oneself to get insular is incredibly crucial—perhaps the most important thing, I think, as a CEO," Tim Cook remarked in an interview with Businessweek.

Being modest will earn you the respect of your staff and is an essential attribute to being a successful leader. Strong leaders must be able to recognize when they are mistaken and confess it in order to move ahead. Tim Cook is a firm believer in owning up to mistakes. Mr. Cook spoke to Businessweek about Steve Jobs' capacity to accept mistakes.

"Perhaps the most underappreciated aspect of Steve was his guts to alter his viewpoint," Cook remarked.

And you should know that it's a skill. It's a gift. This is a powerful leadership lesson about having the fortitude to confess when you're wrong and learning from your errors. Apple is a firm established on the principle of doing what they do well. Apple only makes a few things, which may come as a shock to some. This concentration, according to Tim Cook, is critical to Apple's long-term success. Cook is patient and realizes that fresh and original ideas will emerge. Meanwhile, Apple concentrates on refining its foundation and the goods that consumers enjoy. To actually be a great leader, you must have faith in yourself and trust that your judgments are correct. Your behavior must also reflect your confidence, which is a crucial characteristic of Tim Cook. Many people are unaware of Tim Cook's confidence in his ability to make the best decision.

According to Fox Business, Mr. Cook elected to lose up to one-third of his stock-based remuneration (roughly $130 million over eight years) if Apple's stock underperformed the S&P 500. He opted to lead by example and put his money where his mouth is, so there was no small print. You don't have to give up who you are in the process of being successful as a leader. Being loyal to yourself and being the same person can assist you in becoming a successful leader. Because of his calm and quiet demeanor, many people thought Tim Cook didn't have the necessary mentality to succeed as Apple CEO. He has, nevertheless, demonstrated that he is the right guy for the position. While Steve Jobs was a much more forceful person, Tim Cook has remained loyal to himself and is completing the job with his own skills. Tim Cook understands the need for openness in order to achieve long-term success. After getting scathing criticism regarding Apple's worldwide employee standards, Steve decided to open the doors to the public and let them see how the company operates.

By doing so, he created trust in the company's employees and established new industry standards for manufacturers worldwide.

"With supply responsibility, we aim to be as inventive as we are with our goods." That's a high bar to clear. Cook told Businessweek that "the more transparent we are, the more it's in the public space."

Transparency is an important aspect of leadership. His leadership style is wonderful, and his teachings may teach us all how to lay a strong foundation as a family. With the Mac, iPod, iPhone, iPad, and Apple Watch, Apple has made significant contributions to the creation of market-breaking goods. Each of these items was not the first in their genre, but they each became multibillion-dollar enterprises in their own categories after becoming new divisions in personal computing. Apple is on course to become the world's first three trillion-dollar business, thanks to these gadgets and its services section. Cook has not provided the type of ground-breaking revolutionary products that Steve Jobs did during his leadership role at Apple, but I believe he has made three significant contributions to the firm after Jobs' death in 2011. The first significant contribution he made was in bringing stability to the organization well before Steve Jobs' death. Cook moved in to assuage Wall Street fears about Apple without Steve Jobs as early as 2009, when Jobs stepped down from day-to-day management. After Steve Jobs' death, Cook's strong leadership became even more vital. My phone filled up with calls from national TV networks, big business periodicals, and a slew of local TV and radio stations shortly after the news broke that Jobs had died.

Apple is now worth $2.702.93 billion and is expected to be worth $3 trillion by 2022.In terms of financial performance, Tim Cook's leadership is regarded as one of the major success stories of this century thus far, with Wall Street and investors alike applauding Apple's ongoing innovation and growth even after Steve Jobs' death. The second key contribution is Apple's management style evolution over the previous ten years. During this period, Apple restructured its teams around specialized project managers, whose duty it is to oversee the project from start to finish. There aren't any silos here. This is a significant event. Cook and upper management provide visionary guidance, funding, people, and tools to their product leaders to ensure the project's success. While these project managers report to senior leaders, they have the independence they need to ensure their project's success.

It's easy to imagine the worst-case scenario when dealing with the unknown, but there's always the risk that the person you're dealing with may respond differently than you expect. Have you ever stayed up late practising what you're going to say only for the discussion to take a completely different turn? You have no idea what will happen. Worrying about every potential what-if just adds to your stress level and achieves very little. It's also critical to keep things in perspective. When you're dreading a conversation, it might feel as if the stakes are sky-high. In actuality, if a discussion goes wrong, it may be uncomfortable or produce an unsatisfactory outcome.

Power Points

- To develop credibility, you must be a trusted source of knowledge and decision-making among your team members.
- People want to work under leaders that inspire them while also providing stability and the capacity to shift direction when required.
- Credibility is earned by doing what you say you'll do and standing up for what's right.
- Leaders should not only speak but also behave in order to generate trust and appreciation.
- Good leadership requires the ability to make informed and strategic decisions.
- Last but not least, your mental processes are a vital aspect of embodying leadership.

CHAPTER THREE

BUILDING TRUST AND COHESIVENESS

Learn How To Demonstrate Vulnerability-Based Trust And Become A More Effective Leader.

"A person who is happy is not because everything is right in his life, He is happy because his attitude towards everything in his life is right." - Sundar Pichai

In order to inspire people to adopt new attitudes, you must first accept your own. You all have both good and bad thoughts. Understanding where and when you play, as well as understanding certain triggers, can help you achieve your full potential in the future. Consider what occurs when you meet someone who is better than you in an area where you take pride in yourself and what ideas come to mind. What makes you believe you ended up there? And how does your leadership style reflect that state? This kind of understanding will offer you the ability to name such personalities as well as the will to defeat those myths that are working against you.

- *Are you in a position in your present employment to motivate individuals or groups to take action?*
- *What about incentives?*
- *Are you rewarded for achieving personal or team goals?*

Because humans have a natural desire to put themselves or their group ahead of others, getting teams to collaborate effectively is difficult. Collective influence, on the other hand, necessitates a high level of commitment and effort from all team members. It's much more challenging when people aren't acknowledged or rewarded for driving group action. A communal attitude emphasizes mutual accountability and sharing of results.

Rather than the borders that divide organizations, ideas, and locations, it analyzes links between parts and wholes, stability and change, logic and creativity. It embraces variety by embracing differences, recognizing seeming opposites as interconnected, and gathering evidence from many perspectives. As a result, leaders with a collective attitude give a safe haven for diversity, honouring both individuality and neutrality while encouraging peer cohesiveness. Although it may seem counterintuitive, there are techniques to foster a common attitude inside a company.

To begin, you must focus everyone's attention on a single goal. A unified vision must be shared by all involved. An awareness of how specific problem-solving will benefit them individually and collectively. Second, you'll need to use the same measurements. The manner in which success will be defined, assessed, and reported must be agreed upon by all participants. Third, you must create activities that are mutually reinforcing. Relational is, in my opinion, equally as vital as rational. If you want to develop a collective attitude, you must devote effort to fostering cross-group collaboration. Similarly, continual communication is required to maintain trust and motivation. The impulse to seek and claim credit for all work is one of the most significant hurdles to a communal attitude.

Growth Mindset

These days, the term *"mindset"* is frequently used, but what precisely is a *"mindset"*? A mentality is a set of beliefs that influence how you think. Your thoughts shape the way you approach life and guide all of your decisions and behaviours. A growth mindset is the concept that by putting up effort and devotion, your fundamental talents may be enhanced and improved. When you have a growth mindset, you lean into the needed work to expand your potential in the ways you wish to see it come to life. On the other hand, a fixed mindset is the assumption that your talents are predetermined and cannot be altered. You will avoid difficulties if you have a fixed attitude because you don't want to be embarrassed or humiliated in front of others.

This might be troublesome since your fear of making errors may cause you to shun new challenges and experiences that could help you grow and share your potential with others. A growth mindset, on the other hand, might help you focus on the opportunities ahead of you and find greater joy in the process since you already know you value learning and discovery over what others think of you. The benefits of maintaining a growth mindset have been shown by research. Your muscles relax, you breathe easier, and your inner capacity expands dramatically when you adopt this approach. There are other advantages for the company. When you approach possibilities with an open mind, you become more collaborative, and your collective resilience strengthens over time, since your enthusiasm is contagious.

So, as a leader, how can you transition from a fixed to a growth mindset?

First and foremost, learn to listen to your inner critic. Every time you begin a new activity or assume a new responsibility, that little voice in your head will question, *"Are you sure you can do this?"*

It's up to you to decide how you think and feel. It is also up to you how you perceive the problems, obstacles, and barriers you face. You will uncover undiscovered strength in your resolve if you focus on adjusting your mentality and showing some willpower and retaliate against your inner critic. When you're in a bind, strive to remember your fundamental mission. Consider who you are, who you want to be, and what you want to achieve. The impulse to seek and claim credit for all work is one of the most significant hurdles to a communal attitude. Sharing credit as a role model may be a powerful signal for building internal coalitions. Maintaining an open line of communication can also help to build trust. Finally, focusing on adaptable work can be beneficial. Participants can hunt for additional materials and share ideas by going through the feedback loops you've discovered. As a result, it organizes reactions to promote cohesiveness and trust.

Are you in a position in your present employment to motivate individuals or groups to take action?

What about incentives?

Are you rewarded for achieving personal or team goals?

Because humans have a natural desire to put themselves or their group ahead of others, getting teams to collaborate effectively is difficult. Collective influence, on the other hand, necessitates a high level of commitment and effort from all team members. It's much more challenging when people aren't acknowledged or rewarded for driving group action. A communal attitude emphasises mutual accountability and sharing of results. Rather than the borders that divide organizations, ideas, and locations, it analyzes links between parts and wholes, stability and change, logic and creativity. Connect to your mission and take a genuine action step forward from there. Despite popular belief, leadership is now more about being a particular way than it is about doing something effectively. The more you can model being open-minded for others, the more you can create an environment in which they can be themselves and conditions in which they can grow together.

Collective Attitude

It embraces variety of differences, recognizing seeming opposites as interconnected, and gathering evidence from many perspectives. As a result, leaders with a collective attitude give a safe haven for diversity, honouring both individuality and neutrality while encouraging peer cohesiveness. Although it may seem counterintuitive, there are techniques to foster a common attitude inside a company. To begin, you must focus everyone's attention on a single goal. A unified vision must be shared by all involved. An awareness of how specific problem-solving will benefit them individually and collectively. Second, you'll need to use the same measurements. The manner in which success will be defined, assessed, and reported must be agreed upon by all participants. Third, you must create activities that are mutually reinforcing. It is really beneficial to comprehend how you can best support someone while taking into account various views in order to develop an appropriate support strategy. Being in a position of leadership now is a blessing. You have the ability to shape one's world on a daily basis. Ride the waves and share the happiness. When you can care for, cure, connect, and grow as leaders in the workplace, life becomes so much better for so many more of you.

Once you've broken those links, you'll be more equipped to manage complex and difficult circumstances as a leader. From there, if you notice someone being held back by a dominating attitude, examine what chances for development and learning there could be and consider asking the following questions to increase awareness with the other person.

- *So, as a major team member, what kind of influence or legacy do you want to leave?*
- *Which is more important to you: encouraging heroism or ensuring that everyone has an equal opportunity to develop?*
- *In this case, do you want to contribute to the quarrel or to productivity?*

- *To release innovation, do you believe you should embody diversity of thought or groupthink as a group?*

Creative Thinking

The capacity to come up with feasible answers to issues, convert them into opportunities, and innovate is fueled by a creative mentality. These attributes are seen in people who have a creative attitude. They overcome self-doubt and have faith in their capacity to handle problems. They can deal with ambiguity and complexity because they are adaptive and versatile. They're interested in and open to experimentation, surprise, and discovery. They're willing to take chances and learn from their mistakes.

The finest leaders provide an example for others to follow. As a leader, the greatest first step in creating an environment that includes practises, tools, habits, and a culture that nurtures and supports a more creative staff is to adopt a creative mindset yourself. But don't worry if you don't know where to start; in this course, I'll show you a four-step technique for developing a creative mindset. To begin to trust yourself and your creativity, you'll need to make a mindset shift to overcome the mental hurdles to creativity produced by the inner critic and the prevalent work culture. Then, through embracing and growing curiosity and surprise, as well as enabling flow, you'll seek to spark your inner creativity. After that, you'll develop your creativity talents by learning advanced creative problem-solving techniques.

Companies value creativity above all else in their workers, but how many of you as leaders invest in your own creative development? I begin by discussing how to cultivate a creative-thinking attitude, overcome perfectionism, and establish a basis for enhancing creative thinking. I'll show you how to rekindle your creative flame and improve your creative problem-solving skills. Finally, I'll show you how to instil creative confidence in yourself and your team. By honing your creativity-thinking abilities, you may become a connected and trusted role model capable of sparking change that alters workplaces for the better.

What do you believe this would mean for yourself, your team, and your organization?

I'll tell you what would be different. You'd be better at problem-solving in a creative way. Sharing and cooperation in your teams would improve, and the quantity of unique ideas would grow. Individual and group morale would improve, and people would begin to develop self-confidence and realise their full potential. As your company's products and services improve, you'll come to trust yourself more as a leader. What was the catalyst for all of this? because you've adopted a more creative attitude.

While you may recognize that creativity is vital for both you and your company, you may not be aware of the studies and research that back up this assertion. It all boils down to appreciating the value of creativity. You'll learn about the link between leadership and creativity, as well as why creativity is a talent that should be nurtured at all levels of your company. What is the significance of this? because it has the potential to instil a creative mindset in your organization's culture, ethos, and practises. This will create the groundwork for how you, as a leader, may begin the process of cultivating a creative mindset on a personal level before moving on to a group level.

More and more businesses are confronted with problems that cannot be solved in the usual manner. Businesses' operating conditions are becoming increasingly variable and unpredictable, necessitating ingenuity. The capacity to come up with fresh and significant ideas by using creativity, imagination, and originality. Challenges to current assumptions and the abandonment of inflexible old institutions are driven by creativity and leadership. Leaders need creativity to handle the ever-changing challenges of an uncertain future. Creative leaders encourage success by driving innovation and productivity, allowing businesses to develop cutting-edge goods and services. However, inventiveness isn't limited to those in positions of leadership.

According to the LinkedIn Learning Workplace Learning Report, employees' most desired soft talent is creativity. This is a crucial component for both business and creativity. Hiring more creative individuals as a fast fix won't work if the corporate culture doesn't encourage them. As leaders, you must commit to creating an atmosphere in which creativity is engrained at all levels of business, with a creative mindset as the beginning point.

Indeed, several studies conducted over the last decade reveal that creativity has not only increased in relevance but has also become a must in the workplace. Modern company issues may be turned into opportunities with the right leadership and personnel, but there's a catch. At all levels of business, traditional work culture is at war with creativity. Work for many individuals is packed with monotonous, uninteresting duties, time limitations owing to unrealistic efficiency expectations, and multitasking, all of which kill creativity. Furthermore, stress and worry impede or even prohibit the mental connections that underpin the development of new ideas by dampening brain activity.

Micromanager Or Capability Builder

What if I told you that excellent leadership involves authenticity, understanding, and owning who you are?

The most effective leaders I've worked with are extremely self-aware and open about their peculiarities. Instead of striving to be someone they aren't, they work with and around their skills and flaws. As a consequence, they're more relaxed, confident, and committed to their teams and purpose. I'll show you why hiding who you are will work against you and how to instead look honestly at your situation and work with it. Have you ever felt like you weren't cut out for leadership or that you couldn't be yourself in your current position? Here are a few:

You don't fit your definition of what a leader should be like. There are times when you don't know what to do. You wish to hide anxieties, shortcomings, or holes in your skill set, or you have impostor syndrome and don't believe you're qualified to lead. Do any of these ring true for you? It's natural to feel strained by your job, but if you're continually operating under the notion that you can't be yourself in order to be productive and accepted, you're undercutting yourself. This is why. When you radiate insecurity, it has an impact on how others see you and interact with you. If you don't believe in yourself, others are less inclined to believe in you.

People can tell when you're being honest with them and when you aren't. Putting on a show does not inspire confidence or trust. You're not performing your job if you avoid circumstances that make you uncomfortable. You're not getting stuff done because you're wasting energy on worry and uncertainty. In reality, managing an organization while maintaining a veneer or feeling awful about your perceived flaws is far less effective than leading with honesty and self-assurance. So, what are your options? This is where I suggest you begin. To begin, evaluate your strengths and weaknesses. Take a close look. Pay attention to what others are saying. Be true to yourself.

Solicit feedback from friends, coworkers, or your boss. Next, if you lack expertise in a certain area, either gain the abilities yourself or seek cover from another team member. Remember that being at ease with people who are more knowledgeable than you is not a sign of weakness. It's a show of authority. Finally, be aware of and accept your peculiarities. Everyone has characteristics that are out of the ordinary. Thank you for joining the human race. Make yourself at ease with it. The bottom line is that effective leadership requires self-awareness and acceptance of one's own identity. You're leading from a position of strength when you're totally involved with the people and issues you're there to solve rather than focusing on appearances.

You've all seen the manager who can't trust his or her employees, watches over them too much, and demands continuous and comprehensive briefings. No one wants to work under such a tyrant. But what if you're the micromanager in question? By explaining what inspires them, I'll show you how to avoid becoming a micromanager by explaining what inspires them. Micromanagers, for starters, do not trust people to accomplish their work without supervision. This originates from a lack of faith in their own abilities as well as the abilities of their teams. When you don't know your people's capabilities, you don't know how much they can manage or where the risks are, and if you're not confident in your execution, any slip-ups may be disastrous.

So you hover over your team, checking in on every step in the hopes of avoiding a blunder and, as a result, suffocating your contributions. This has the potential to be a big morale killer. The solution is to get to know your coworkers. Learn about each person's strengths, limitations, and objectives. Take a look at what they've done previously. Recognize what makes people tick. Provide training if there are any skills shortages. If there are any difficulties with performance, fix them. You'll eventually figure out where your team's zone of excellence is, and you'll be able to trust them to accomplish their jobs. Micromanagers also lack the ability to delegate. If you don't know how to delegate jobs properly, you'll be hovering over your employees, monitoring their every move and even performing part of the work yourself.

Delegate Not Relegate

The key is to learn how to delegate effectively. Clarify responsibilities, get consensus, encourage your team, and hold them accountable for their stated commitments. Delegating allows you to focus on higher-level projects while also allowing your team to grow and develop. Micromanagers seldom let their staff decide how to solve an issue, preferring instead to tell them what to do. It's your role as a leader to ensure that everyone understands the business context and goals for their work. This is the reason It's also your responsibility to ensure that everyone understands the final result and the desired outcome of their effort. This is the situation. The how, on the other hand, is the realm of your team's contributors.

You're micromanaging if you're constantly telling employees how to do their tasks. The key is to learn how to train your employees. Instead of telling them what to do, empower them to own their work, define the problem's boundaries, and come up with their own solutions. Micromanagers degrade morale, limit the progress of their teams, and squander their own time. Get to know your staff, learn to delegate, and coach rather than tell if you don't want to be that boss.

As a leader, one of the most effective ways to develop your employees is to coach them. Allowing them to wrestle with an issue and come up with their own solutions rather than telling them what to do allows them to learn at a deeper level and increases their experience and confidence. I'll guide you through the two most crucial coaching tools you have at your disposal in this lesson. First and foremost, consider your thinking. You want the other person to think freely and creatively as a coach. Entering the conversation with an open mind and a neutral attitude tells the other person that you're interested in hearing what they have to say.

This entails putting your own agenda for how a solution should be arrived at aside, allowing for inquiry without judgement, and being genuinely interested in the other person's ideas. Of course, you'll notice that your thoughts and skills come up during the talk. You solve issues all day, and that portion of your brain isn't going to go away simply because you're having a coaching session. So it's up to you to recognize and dismiss your inner counsel provider. I don't require your assistance at this time. So I'm going to return to coaching.

Powerful questions are another discipline to add to your coaching toolkit. Not every inquiry is the same. These come in a range of shapes and sizes. This is your view with a question mark. Aren't you pleased you went ahead and did it? You're grateful they did it, and you want them to agree with you. The most important question This is your proposal in the form of a question, asking, *"What have you tried?"* It's just your advice to attempt a certain remedy. The yes/no dilemma These are legitimate issues, yet they don't generate much thought or investigation.

A yes-or-no question will provide you with very little information. On the other hand, powerful questions allow for more in-depth, serious contemplation. The fact that they are open-ended and future-oriented is one of their most fundamental characteristics. Examine how you might transform a question from one that is useless to one that generates insight and possibilities. Ask a straightforward yes-or-no question instead of a question that isn't even a question. Instead of a yes-or-no inquiry, start with an open-ended one and then go on to a future-oriented one. After that, go on to an open-ended inquiry, and lastly, offer a truly free-form question to really get the other person thinking. You may improve your coaching skills by practising, creating, and asking compelling questions. You'll be eliciting insights and ideas in no time if you combine them with a neutral and inquiring mentality.

Performance In Uncertainty

It's extremely stressful to feel as if everything is out of your control, and the situation is exacerbated when you're in a position of leadership. You have a lot of people looking to you to guide them through the crisis, and you can't just walk away from it. Those times when everything seems to be going wrong are truly times of chaos. When was the last time you felt completely out of control, that there was no way to solve things, and that the only thing you could do was throw your hands up and walk away? If you're in a position of leadership, that sensation is amplified. You can't just walk away, and a lot of people are counting on you to lead.

It's nearly impossible to escape change weariness in times of instability. So, let me share some ways with you to assist your team in becoming more change resilient. Reevaluate initiatives that are part of a planned change programme first. What other tasks may be postponed or reinvented while the company manages through chaos? Locate them and shift resources and timetables accordingly. This will allow you to avoid making changes that aren't essential at the moment, alleviating the load of change on your personnel. After that, inquire about your team's progress. You may achieve this by conducting a poll in which everyone is asked to describe how they are coping with the present shift. This will provide you with suggestions for how to effectively assist your team.

If people believe that surviving the current situation is impossible, they will find it difficult to come up with novel ideas. As a leader, your first step is to embrace a human-centered approach. This approach places a strong emphasis on your team's overall well-being. Because your focus is on expressing your empathy for your team while they struggle with chaotic conditions affecting their job and personal life, a human-centered mentality builds connection. You must facilitate brainstorming sessions and other talks as a leader in a way that encourages constructive debate about ideas that may appear hard to implement on the surface. Those are the kinds of thoughts that might generate more conversation and lead to the answers you're looking for. And don't limit yourself to team members with certain designations; think of them in terms of how they think. Check to see if your brainstorming and decision-making process includes ideators, clarifiers, developers, and implementers. These are the folks who will assist you in gaining a better grasp of the new uncharted region in which your company must operate.

When not just one thing goes wrong, but everything goes wrong, it's a genuine time of chaos.

But, in this course, I'd want to show you how, even in the midst of chaos and calamity, you can still locate and create order. This book will teach you how to inspire creativity in the face of adversity by studying the characteristics of a creative leader and the creative problem-solving method. I understand that turmoil feels completely out of control, but there is a solution. Everyone's answer will be different, but this course will provide you with the skills you'll need to uncover it.

Today's businesses do not exist in a vacuum. Everything in today's global economy is part of a domino effect. Because PepsiCo is such a significant part of the American economy and the global economy, Nooyi was tasked with making judgments that impacted not only PepsiCo but the whole globe. Her mantra was *"performance with a purpose,"* which she implemented at PepsiCo by shifting the company's operations to healthier and more sustainable choices. In this regard, Nooyi made a number of purchases. One of them was the purchase of health food businesses like Kevita. Because of this innovative technique, PepsiCo was able to cope with decreased sales of fizzy drinks and junk food. Nooyi decreased the sugar, fat, and salt levels in its goods and provided diet alternatives throughout its range as part of the company's goal to reduce obesity rates, with its key products being soda and chips. Her aim was to not just propel PepsiCo ahead, but to propel everyone forward as well. Great leaders have a multi-faceted vision, one that makes you think about something from several perspectives.

Great leaders make decisions with conviction, even when they are scrutinised and criticized. The critics were harsh on Indra Nooyi when she decided to make PepsiCo goods healthier. They advised her to ignore nutrition and concentrate solely on selling more chips and soda. But she was aware of her responsibilities and proceeded with caution. So she persisted, not just making further efforts toward creating healthier and more sustainable goods but also establishing the Healthy Weight Commitment Foundation. As a consequence, their food and beverage items were reduced by 6.4 million calories, exceeding their promise by more than 400% three years ahead of time.Indra's leadership characteristics Nooyi also requires her to be a skilled communicator.

"You can never spend too much on communication skills—both written and spoken," she stated, highlighting the significance of communication skills in being a strong leader.

Activist investors had pushed for a separation of the beverage and Frito-Lay businesses. Nooyi maintained that retaining the two firms under one roof was critical to preserving PepsiCo's position as an industry leader and gaining a competitive edge over other food retailers. She was able to stop the conversations in 2016 because of her persuasive and communication abilities. To be a great leader, you must be a great student, and being a student has no phase or time limit. Great leaders, such as Indra Nooyi, are lifelong students. This is especially crucial in light of the digital society you now live in. Nooyi kept up with emerging technology and fashion trends. Indra Nooyi's ability to listen is one of her most impressive leadership characteristics. She paid attention to her coworkers, subordinates, and customers.

"There are always folks with suggestions for how we may do things differently—ideas we may not want to hear," "But I've discovered that when I'm prepared to listen, I'm a better person as a result.", she said.

More than a simple management education is required of CEOs. It necessitates leaving the workplace and observing things up close. Nooyi was a people-person who absorbed information from all sources. She would meet with government officials and civic leaders, attend workshops to stay up to date on industry developments, speak with field salesmen, and even photograph their items on store shelves.

Authenticity is a quality of creative leaders. Your true passion will attract others who support your cause because of the genuine passion you show through your words and deeds. When you need to discover an imaginative solution to a chaotic circumstance, this coalition of individuals who believe in your vision will become your team. Next, creative leaders are at ease with failure, or as I prefer to refer to it, opportunity. In order to be relevant in business, there is a lot of pressure to be the first or the greatest.

Indra Nooyi is routinely listed as one of the world's most powerful women. A modest individual, a compelling leader, and a role model for many women throughout the world who are attempting to manage work and family life. The leadership characteristics and approach of Indra Nooyi are unusual. She is noted for her *"working together and being completely honest"* leadership approach, as opposed to the *"delegate-foresee-manipulate"* model. The success of Indra and PepsiCo throughout her term is due to the manner in which she led. The leadership traits that made Indra Nooyi such a brilliant leader, as noticed and admired by many, are listed below.

Indra Nooyi's famous phrase, *"Leave your crown in the garage,"* was also a life lesson she received from her mother. She discusses the significance of living the crown in the garage in her piece, which recounts the genesis of the statement.

She writes, "No matter who we are or what we do, nobody can take our place in our families. So, leave the crown in the garage."

Nooyi implemented a set of ideals around sustainability that he believes are vital to PepsiCo's long-term success. ***"Purpose has no negative impact on profitability." "How you drive transformation is via purpose,"*** she wrote in a Harvard Business Review essay. Water consumption, packaging, climate change, and agriculture have all been the subject of operations changes and new design. PepsiCo is active in programmes such as supplying safe drinking water to poor nations, in addition to lowering fuel, power, and water consumption. Her mantra was *"performance with a purpose,"* which she implemented at PepsiCo by shifting the company's operations to healthier and more sustainable choices.

A person who demonstrates creativity perceives a problem differently than others, resulting in new or innovative ideas. It doesn't matter if you're talking about art, music, a corporate product, or a process. Understanding the four Ps of creativity might help you think about creativity more clearly in practise. These four Ps symbolise four things to consider when you're in a chaotic scenario and require a creative solution. The initial letter of the alphabet stands for people. You, of course, are referred to as a person. The person is at the heart of creativity. Your creativity, your capacity to view things in new ways that others haven't. This may appear daunting, but it may be less difficult than you think. You already have a distinct viewpoint and a set of experiences. This implies that you can already come up with a creative solution to a problem. All you have to do now is trust the creative process and let it flow. The following P stands for process. A process is any series of steps that you repeat in the same order every time without skipping any. It's a method for fostering innovation in your company in this scenario. Thinking about developing creative solutions through a structured approach may seem counterintuitive to what you should be doing. That is, however, the beauty of creation.

Indra Nooyi redefined what it means to be an extraordinary leader in this intimate and riveting memoir by the pioneering former CEO of PepsiCo, over a dozen years as one of the world's most renowned CEOs. She revolutionised PepsiCo with a distinctive vision, a rigorous pursuit of excellence, and a profound sense of purpose, becoming the first woman of colour and immigrant to lead a company like pepsi—and one of the leading strategic thinkers of our time. *"My Life in Full"*, a beautiful book bursting with elegance, courage, and good humour, provides a first-hand account of Nooyi's remarkable career and the many sacrifices it took. The book provides an intimate look at PepsiCo and Nooyi's ideas as she led the iconic American corporation toward healthier goods and a new environmental reputation, despite opposition at every turn. For the first time, Nooyi also lays bare the challenges she faced while juggling a busy career and a growing family, as well as what she learnt along the way. She presents a compelling argument for how strengthening corporate and community support for young family builders would unlock the economy's full potential, and she makes a clear, concrete, and urgent plea for business and government to prioritize the care ecosystem, paid leave, and work flexibility. The tale of an outstanding leader's life; a heartfelt homage to the connections that built it; and a plan for 21st-century success. Generous, authoritative, and founded on real experience.

You're combining the powers of inventiveness and discipline, which appear to be at war with one another. To find answers to previously unsolved issues. The following P stands for performance, which is the setting in which a person may see the creative process. As a leader, are you establishing an organizational culture that encourages employees to share their ideas without fear of being judged? Is it true that when an idea receives support, it also receives funding and the human resources required to put it into action? Is it possible for individuals to fail without fear of retaliation? All of these elements must be present in order for creativity to thrive in a given setting. The fourth P stands for productivity. The consequence of the individual who follows the method in an environment that encourages creativity is the productivity. Your productivity is your unique answer to your challenges. Use the four Ps to help you think of new ways to solve problems. The sheer essence of chaos indicates that a large number of unconnected, uncontrollable events are taking place at the same time. You must find order in the chaos in order to find a solution to the chaotic circumstance you are in.

Finally, this is where your ability to make sense will be tested. Take advantage of this chance to lead your team through the sense-making process with the purpose of better understanding your existing environment, what's feasible in that context, and how you can act to change it. Encourage your team to notice and learn from how their decisions affect the environment as you implement the concepts they've agreed on. Then urge them to be adaptable in the face of such changes. The fact that there is no one-size-fits-all answer can make turbulent times even more tough. Being a leader is like riding a violent roller coaster with many ups and downs, twists and turns. And it's during those low points that you search for motivation to keep going. It happens frequently; in fact, it occurs on a regular basis.

Here's Jeff Bezos's obsession with this decision-making style—*"it's his secret to success."* Amazon founder and CEO Jeff Bezos is known for delivering odd, contentious, and yet surprisingly useful advice. When it comes to decision-making, he's particularly obsessed with time and resource constraints. When it came to making important business decisions, Jeff Bezos followed a set of principles that helped him lead Amazon to great success.

Look no farther than the executive teams of certain firms to understand why they have a poisonous culture, underperform relative to their potential, and finally collapse. Incompetent leaders drive worried, alienated people to engage in counterproductive work practises and spread toxicity across the company, whereas competent leaders produce high levels of trust, engagement, and productivity. Consider that avoiding a toxic employee has a two-fold economic impact compared to recruiting a star performer. Low levels of employee engagement, as well as high levels of passive job hunting and self-employment, are mostly due to inept management.In an ideal world, people assessing applicants for leadership positions—in both politics and business—would try to spot possible signs of ineptitude. Culture, whether good or terrible, is the result of our leaders' ideals and practises. As a result, preventing unethical people from getting to the top is the best way to establish a positive one. This is true for both men and women, although we appear to be less concerned with battling ineptitude in men than in women. Of course, hiring managers might make it easier for inept women to become leaders, but a far better option is to discriminate more extensively against incompetent males, who are now underrepresented in leadership positions.

"Leadership to me means duty, honor, country. It means character, and it means listening from time to think we need the feminine qualities of leadership, which include attention to aesthetics and the environment, nurturing, affection, intuition, and the qualities that make people feel safe and cared for." - Deepak Chopra

Power Points

- In order to inspire people to adopt new attitudes, you must first accept your own.
- When you have a growth mindset, you lean into the needed work to expand your potential in the ways you wish to see it come to life.
- Everything in today's global economy is part of a domino effect.

CHAPTER FOUR

TRAP OF PERFECTIONISM

Is Chasing Perfection Hard To Achieve?

"You are not born with a fixed amount of resilience. Like a muscle, you can build it up, draw on it when you need it. In that process you will figure out who you really are — and you just might become the very best version of yourself."-Sheryl Sandberg

Perfectionism, feeling detached from your accomplishments, deflecting praise, feeling that you aren't knowledgeable enough, and believing that your present work function is above the level that you are actually intended to be are all examples of these. This is something you must hear. Even though you feel like one, you are not a fraud. You should also hear this. If you're a member of a historically marginalized or discriminated-against group, such as women, people of colour, or others, your sentiments of impostor syndrome are most likely the result of being perceived as an imposter your whole career. Here's the bad news in terms of inventiveness. You can't access or develop your creativity if you're secretly suffering from impostor syndrome.

Your Challenges

Do you find yourself overcompensating by over-preparing because you're terrified of not knowing enough? Or do you have unrealistically high standards that you must meet? *"I'm not really a leader,"* you may have thought, or *"Someday they'll realise I'm clueless."* If so, you may be suffering from impostor syndrome, a psychological condition in which people refuse to internalize their achievements despite overwhelming evidence to the contrary. Keep an eye out for any other signs of this persistent self-doubt.

If you don't believe you're a phoney, you probably don't have Dunning-Syndrome. Kruger's talented individuals are the ones that suffer from impostor syndrome and are afraid of being discovered as phonies. People with an inflated sense of self are unlikely to fall into this category. The good news is as follows: If you're feeling like an impostor, it's because you're one-of-a-kind.

Because of the strict mindset that underpins perfectionism, it stifles innovation. Flexibility, curiosity, investigation, and learning from so-called mistakes and failures are all required for creativity. How can you improve creatively if you have a concept of what something should be in your thoughts but never manage to make it happen? The idea is to let go of the need to be flawless in order to pave the way for a more creative attitude to emerge.

Excellence vs. perfection is the name given to this creative dosage.

It's critical to recognize and appreciate that perfection is not synonymous with greatness. That's correct. The terms *"perfection" and "excellence"* are not interchangeable.

What's the difference between the two?

In other words, trust me when I say you are not alone in your feelings. The second piece of good news is that impostor syndrome is riddled with contradictions. It's called the impostor syndrome dilemma, and it goes like this: only when you are knowledgeable and talented will you feel impostor syndrome. As many times as you need to, repeat this to yourself. In fact, write it on your mirror or make it your desktop wallpaper to ensure that the message is fully absorbed. To be clear, impostor syndrome is not to be confused with the *"Dunning-Kruger"* effect, also known as competence and competence, in which people incorrectly judge their skill and level of knowledge while failing to acknowledge that they are in fact incompetent.

When you're working on a project, you're more concerned with the end result than with the process. You feel that effort and focus are insufficient. The end result must always be productive and, above all, successful. When things go wrong or you don't meet expectations, you feel like you've failed. You're worried that you won't be able to meet your own standards. You feel that if you keep achieving and looking good while doing it, you will be successful and happy. When you do succeed, though, the happiness is just transient and ephemeral. By becoming your own toughest critic, you aim to beat others to the punch.

"Management is about persuading people to do things they do not want to do, while leadership is about inspiring people to do things they never thought they could." - Steve Jobs

You're acutely aware of situations that can create the impression that you're not flawless, and you covertly evaluate others who fall short of perfection. These are some of the characteristics and expressions of perfectionism, the unattainable pursuit of perfection. If you haven't figured it out yet, impostor syndrome frequently leads to perfectionism. When you feel inadequate in some manner, you push yourselves to be flawless and subject yourselves to impossible standards that you would never set for others. This might lead to you putting your energy and effort into the wrong things, causing you to work in fits and spurts, exhausting yourselves and running yourselves into the ground.

Striving for greatness is actively seeking out situations from which you can learn and appreciate, and then growing skills, confidence, and finally mastery as a result of those experiences. Striking for perfection, on the other hand, sometimes leads to bad sentiments as a result of not achieving a specific degree of success and then being too critical of your performance and perceived flaws.

There's a beautiful Aristotle phrase that states, "We are what we do over and over again. Excellence, then, is a habit, not an act."

Allow yourself to practise at whatever you're doing to work on developing excellence and overcoming perfectionism. By practising, you begin to develop the activity's habit, which will eventually lead to greatness. Keep reminding yourself that the aim is greatness, not perfection, as you work to improve your own creativity, talents, and knowledge, and then enjoy the process.

Finally, you'll ensure that your teams are more creative by enhancing connection, communication, and creative confidence. To be able to allow the brilliant thoughts within your mind to come out, you need to grow and enhance your concentration and attention. However, if a loud inner critic is causing you to dwell on feelings of being an impostor, striving for perfection, or sustaining a fixed worldview, your creativity will be stifled. Now is the moment to embrace your inner artist. To get there, you'll focus on removing mental barriers to creative thinking and replacing them with significant mindset modifications that will pave the way for more innovative thinking and a blooming imagination.

Creative Minds

Being creative isn't about having a lot of skills; it's about opting to accept and harness what you currently have and then using that framework to solve creative problems. You may, on the other hand, feel that talents such as creativity, skill, and intellect are set, immutable characteristics. If this is the case, it will be quite difficult to believe that one may grow and develop creativity.

According to the author, "Creativity isn't one of your skills , it's how you choose to go about things."

In order to improve your creative thinking, you must first consider your attitude. People with a fixed mentality are more concerned with recording their intellect or skill than with growing it. They also believe that talent, rather than hard work, is what leads to success. A fixed mindset inner voice is, by the way, the same as the inner critic. A growth mindset, on the other hand, emphasises learning, willingness to fail, curiosity, expansion, and self-reflection. People who have a growth mindset think that their most fundamental talents can be enhanced through hard effort and devotion, and that intelligence and ability are just the beginning. Learning to be self-referential, curiosity, growth, and a willingness to fail are all attributes that are part of being creative. Ask yourself these questions to figure out which side of the attitude fence you're on.

- *Do I shy away from challenges, or do I embrace them?*
- *Do I give up easily when faced with challenges, or do I persevere?*
- *Do I perceive effort as a waste of time or as a means to mastery?*
- *Do I disregard or learn from constructive criticism or negative feedback?*
- *Do I see other people's success as a threat or an opportunity to learn from and be inspired by it?*

Don't despair if you find yourself leaning toward the fixed mentality camp; there are strategies to transition to a development mindset. To shift from a fixed to a development mindset, follow these steps.

- Step one is to become aware of your stuck mentality voice. If you find yourself thinking about perfectionism or fear of failure, recognise that it's your fixed mentality talking.
- The second step is to acknowledge that you have a choice. You aren't condemned to think this way for the rest of your life. When you wish to modify anything, your brain and mind are extremely adaptive.
- Step three is to respond to it in a development mindset manner. Transform your language to be more self-supportive and

curious.

- Step four is to implement the following growth mindset strategies: First and foremost, keep a beginner's mind. Free yourself from the expert's tyranny and ask yourself, *"Isn't this interesting?"*

Rediscover the familiar and pay greater attention to your surroundings. You may even make it a treasure hunt to see what's fresh and fascinating. Another option is to learn something new from a buddy. Number three, broaden your horizons by learning something new. Rekindle your enthusiasm for learning and prepare yourself to thrive in the face of difficulty and change. Number four, fail ahead, and ask questions to fill up the holes in your understanding. Learn from your errors and don't be afraid to admit that you made a mistake because you were weak in some way. Reflect on your experience to have a better understanding of how to modify and build resilience as you work toward your objectives. For both yourself and others, adopting a growth mentality will pave the way for the development of a healthy creative mindset.

When you get jaded, make presumptions and assumptions, and stop seeing things with fresh eyes, creativity dies or remains undeveloped. However, research shows that unexpected events often lead to innovative ideas. It turns out that the element of unpredictability encourages divergent thinking, or the generation of a large number of ideas in a short amount of time. Furthermore, additional research demonstrates that highly creative people have fewer cognitive filters and exhibit cognitive disinhibition.

This means they absorb a lot of knowledge and subtleties that most people would overlook, providing them with a rich mental treasure from which to draw when creating creative correlations. You must learn to build new attention habits in order to nurture a creative mentality. You'll need to learn multiple ways to look at things and how to look at them differently. You must begin to think new ideas and feel new sentiments about what you are experiencing. You may do all of this by looking for unexpected opportunities. Surprisingly, the element of surprise may be deliberately engineered into your life to fuel your increasing creative mentality.

Constraints, rather than limiting creativity, stimulate it. This finding contradicts the widely held belief that you can only be creative and inventive if you have boundless resources. It turns out that a lack of limitations encourages complacency and poor thinking. Without any limits, you are more likely to choose the mental path of least resistance, going to the first thing that comes to mind, which is frequently based on what is already well-known or familiar. Constraints, on the other hand, create a sense of challenge, concentration, and direction. When you're working with limits, you're more likely to create unexpected connections and come up with fresh ideas.

With limits, you're forced to identify the best idea rather than going with the initial one. In order to accomplish so, you need to access additional information from your mental databases. I'm sure you're already convinced that working with restrictions leads to stronger ideas, products, and outcomes. How can you set limits that will force you and your team to reach the higher levels of creativity you desire? How do you design the greatest box that encourages you to think beyond the lines? Part of the trick is to frame the limitations as opportunities, as challenges that will help you to be more creative. There are a few different methods to make anything.

To begin, set a budget for resources, such as output material or media, tools, topics, human power, and timescale. After that, you may put processes, procedures, guidelines, or policies in place. Make it obvious which limitations are critical and which are great to have once you've established your constraints. See what types of concepts you can come up with when you operate under these new constraints. A word of warning, though: Constraints are really beneficial, but only up to a point. When limits grow too tight, instead of encouraging creativity and invention, they suffocate them, leaving most individuals disheartened. Always be on the alert as a leader for when restrictions become a barrier rather than a fuel for innovation and master coordinating the many sorts of constraints for the greatest results.

Functional Formula

As a manager, you have the ability to create or destroy your workers' work experience. This book will show you how to improve your leadership abilities, develop a team vision, and eventually progress from a manager to an inspirational leader. Learn how to delegate and motivate employees, communicate effectively, deal with difficult individuals, and prepare for the future of your company. Along the way, the author uses examples from a variety of sectors to demonstrate how these principles work in practise. Some of history's greatest leaders have been charismatic, yet charisma is something that cannot be taught. But the good news is that most of you who are just in charge of people at work, who have recently become bosses, do not require charm. You may learn to motivate others. It is critical to be motivated. And it would be wonderful if there was a lot of motivation, which you could term inspiration. People who are merely going through the motions, doing what they're told to be paid, will never be great. They'll never be able to outperform the competition, and they'll never be able to love their jobs. And I believe that most companies suffer from a severe lack of desire.

Most managers I see and have worked for in the past appear to rely on force and compulsion, or they just issue orders. And if you're a boss, why do anything else if you know your employees are obligated to follow your orders? And other bosses are simply non-existent most of the time; you only see them when you're in difficulty. Other employers appear to believe that their duty is just to keep you in line, to criticise you when you make mistakes, or to keep an eye on you. But these employers are missing out on a lot since their employees could do so much more if they cared, if they were motivated, if they were engaged.

As a result, inspiring leadership or management is critical, and it is something that can be learned. If you look at the history of management theory, you'll see that there was once a concept known as trait theory. It's now generally discredited, but the concept was that you'd look at legendary leaders throughout history and effective leaders in your own firm to figure out what the best ones do. So, in a sense, characteristic theory has faded, and you've come to understand that there are many alternative ways to execute a job. The good news for your ordinary mortals, I believe, is that charm isn't required to be a successful manager, boss, or leader. And that's a comfort since charm isn't something you can learn.

Simple things like speaking with people, setting clear goals for them, concentrating on the good, and appreciating their work. It's all simple stuff that you can do, but few bosses really do it. Which is fantastic because you have a genuine opportunity to be better than average, if not one of the best bosses in the industry. The inspiring leader is a manager as well as a leader. And I believe that most managers should be able to do both. They have to be able to do both. So, how can you tell the difference between a manager and a leader? Management is more about structure, planning, and control, but leadership is more about vision, communication, and motivation. So, leaders must do some planning and organising, and managers must do some motivating, and in a perfect world, you would be able to do both. As a result, if you're a manager, you must also be a leader.

Leaders should focus on people's talents rather than their flaws while directing the game. A leader's short and long-term vision must be crystal clear. It may be difficult to build a long-term vision without enough data points, but the capacity to foresee and construct scenarios using those data points is critical. To achieve buy-in as a leader, you must communicate effectively. It can only happen if you create an atmosphere in which everyone can look at your idea and say, *"Yes, this is where I need to be, or where I want to be."* People may regard you differently as a leader at various times. Still, in order to adapt to the situational management style, one must receive input and adjust; therefore, flexibility is essential. Second, even when you don't have enough data points, having a clear vision is critical. By communicating that vision and gaining buy-in, one may achieve the goals while using people's capabilities.

A role model is an inspirational leader. This is because your teammates keep a far closer eye on you than you know. They're always looking at what you're doing, and they're going to imitate it. And, as someone told me not long ago, the problem is that they imitate bad things far more than positive. So anything you do that isn't good, they'll all duplicate it. And they're always keeping an eye on you. It's a frightening concept, but it's a fact of life; you're a role model, and you have to be flawless all of the time, or as close to it as possible. So, what would they be on the lookout for? What kinds of things should you do? Well, first of all, be approachable.

Elon Musk's leadership style emphasizes continuous learning, breaking down obstacles, and creating novel approaches to challenges. He also has the emotional intelligence to get the best out of his staff, and you can credit his enormous success to all of this. He has, however, been chastised for being a workaholic and an overbearing micromanager, both of which are bad leadership characteristics. Finally, the best leaders focus their efforts on inspiring their employees to be better so that they may all contribute to the company's success. Perhaps this is what Musk's approach is missing. Musk appears to get one thing right: his commitment to ongoing development.

Elon Musk's leadership skills are exciting, but they also have the potential to be poisonous. He, like Steve Jobs, is renowned for his brilliance, but that doesn't change the fact that he's famously tough to deal with. This is due to the fact that he exhibits traits of both an autocratic and a transactional leader. If left uncontrolled, these two leadership styles can cause major organizational issues. Musk, on the other hand, isn't a cruel, task-oriented tyrant; instead, he's preoccupied with producing exceptional outcomes. The employee admitted that the process was difficult but that they emerged *"ten times smarter."*

Dealing With Failure

Elon Musk's revolutionary, dictatorial, and transactional leadership style demonstrates that he is in business to make money, not friends. He expects greatness since it is what propels change. Elon Musk has had his share of setbacks. Around the holidays in 2008, he was on the verge of losing both Tesla and SpaceX. Even in the face of adversity, he displayed exceptional leadership qualities that inspired his team to keep moving forward. A failure in leadership would have devastated you not just from the perspective of the press or prospective consumers, but it would have destroyed you inside, Knowing this, Musk gave a motivational speech to his staff, describing their purpose and the fact that they will succeed. You may even produce a guidebook for your organization on how to deal with failure.

Another excellent method is to lead by example. Demonstrate how to take responsibility for mistakes and pivot away from setbacks for your team. Destigmatize the shame that comes with failing to create a safe atmosphere for failure. Discuss why failure is important and how it may lead to progress, growth, and innovation. Additionally, consider strategies to improve and establish channels of communication about missteps. Make it a point to lead this activity by revealing your personal setbacks and how you overcame them.

Elon Musk is a visionary who believes wholeheartedly in every commercial endeavour he embarks on. He isn't frightened to tackle hurdles that others would deem hard to conquer since he has such a clear vision. From automotive to telecommunications to energy, the initiatives he's worked on have touched practically every major business and global issue. And you can bet that if there's an issue within the company, Musk will be right there to assist in finding a solution: *"I relocate to wherever the most serious issue in Tesla is."*

Elon Musk is one of the most successful leaders of current time, despite the controversy that surrounds him. But what is it about him that makes him so successful? You look at five things he can teach all about how to lead effectively. And, while he obviously enjoys putting himself at the centre of problems, it's crucial not to overlook the benefits of sharing risks, ideas, and decision-making with your entire team in genuine adaptive leadership style. You will not only accelerate the success of the business, but you will also generate a more engaged and happy workforce by enabling everyone in the organization to overcome challenges on their own.

He not only invites others to give him constructive input, but he also encourages his staff to do so. He believes that honest feedback has the capacity to improve individual, team, and organizational performance:

"I believe it is critical to establish a feedback loop in which you are always thinking about what you've done and how you may improve."

That, you believe, is the single finest piece of advice: continually question yourself and consider how you may be doing things better. Never make a decision based on a one-size-fits-all approach. Many decisions are two-way reversible doors. A light-weight approach can be used to make those judgments. The majority of decisions should be made with roughly 70% of the information you wish you had. In most circumstances, if you wait for 90%, you're probably being sluggish. Being wrong may be less costly than you think if you're good at course correction, whereas being slow will be costly. You will save a lot of time if you use the term *"disagree and commit."* It's helpful to say, *"Look, I know we disagree on this, but will you gamble with me on it?"* if you're passionate about a particular direction despite the lack of consensus. Disagree and make a commitment? By the time you reach this step, no one can be certain, thus you'll most likely receive a hasty yes. Recognize and escalate real misalignment concerns as soon as possible.

Teams can have conflicting goals and fundamentally opposing viewpoints. They simply aren't on the same page — and no amount of discussion or meetings will fix that fundamental misalignment. Exhaustion is the default dispute resolution mechanism in this scenario if escalation is not used. The decision is made by whoever has the most stamina. Because they're continually asking whether you're allowed to speak with them. And I believe you are more afraid of your superiors than you know. So, if you're a boss and you believe you're accessible, keep in mind that you could not be. Unapproachable implies you can't go visit someone even if you're busy. As a result, make sure you're not a terrifying boss. Be approachable at all times. The third rule is to never get furious and to always remain cool and cheerful in the face of errors, even if they have just deleted everything on the computer.

Don't make personal attacks on the individual and don't dismiss them as ineffective. Simply state gently that this is okay and this is not. As a result, everyone is aware of the regulations. Also tied to this is the need to maintain a cheerful attitude. You can do it, and if something goes wrong, you can repair it. If there's a major objective that you're all attempting to attain, you'll be able to accomplish it. They're all trying to be like you, and they're all watching to see if you're positive or not. So you must believe, and I believe it is difficult to perform and seem optimistic if you don't believe. As a result, you must truly think that you are capable of completing the task. The information will subsequently be sent to your team. So, before you even start talking to people, have a good mindset. Another thing they're always on the lookout for is what you concentrate on. As a result, always look on the bright side of things. You'll go through this in further depth later.

It was a huge accomplishment in and of itself to introduce the world to online shopping when it was still science fiction. This far-fetched notion of purchasing and selling products online appeared impossible, yet, as you all know, Amazon is now one of the most popular e-commerce sites. It wasn't easy for Jeff Bezos to beat the odds, but his leadership beliefs helped him win the lottery. From a fresh viewpoint in the business world, from altering people's thinking to changing the way they purchase.

The most important leadership philosophy adopted by Jeff Bezos was that of his customers and employees. He thought that the client should be treated as a king. Additionally, in order to keep corporate stockholders informed about the company's success and values, Jeff Bezos began an unusual yet effective method of issuing shareholder letters. As CEO of Amazon, Jeff Bezos brought several changes to the organization, but one of the most notable is the workplace culture. It wasn't simple to create a joyful environment for consumers and employees, but Amazon was able to do it because of Jeff Bezos' leadership style.

Jeff Bezos thinks that in order to be successful, one must first focus on the client. He also displayed it in a unique manner during meetings. Because the client was unable to attend a meeting, he always maintained an empty chair in the conference room to symbolise the customer. This was done to persuade the team to come up with customer-friendly solutions and ideas. Jeff Bezos, as a leader, believes in long-term thinking and outcomes in a world when everyone is focused on short-term profit. Amazon's top services, like as the Kindle, Amazon Web Services, and Amazon Prime, would not have existed if he had been focused on short-term goals, he claims. This strategy provided Amazon and Bezos an advantage over their rivals.

The desire to experiment is what distinguishes a successful firm from an unsuccessful one. You can't have invention without failure, as Jeff stated in an interview. Amazon as a firm performs and supports experimenting, which helps them to develop the products you see today. Additionally, Jeff feels that the majority of inventions are the result of trial and error, which is a component of the experimental process. Bezos feels that holding meetings and talks in small groups saves time and effort in terms of establishing a framework.For group talks, whether inside the team or throughout the organization, he instituted the "two pizza rule."

Jeff Bezos thinks that in order to create anything big and meaningful, you must have a clear vision and the determination to stick to it. He claims that you must be flexible with the process while maintaining a firm vision of the final objective. There will be a lot of experimentation and mistakes along the way, and in order to correct them, you'll need to have a flexible mentality. Jeff Bezos is known for being a game-changer in the e-commerce business, a role model for Amazon employees, and owning thriving enterprises all over the world. Do you aspire to be more like him and learn from his experiences?

Employees and firms must adapt, embrace, and adopt initiatives that promote productivity and teamwork in the face of increased competition and dynamic changes. This strategy allows Amazon to maintain a high-performing business culture while still keeping its employees satisfied. The "two pizza rule" said that every conversation or team gathering should be limited to groups of 5 to 7 persons who could finish two pizzas. This is part of Bezos' distinctive leadership style, which says that having more people in a conversation reduces productivity.

When you tap into your team's potential, you can accomplish greatness. You've probably heard this expression.The leader, the one who sets the standards, is frequently the source of brilliance in a successful team. The finest leaders take a step back and let their team members do what they do best. Control leads to conformity, while autonomy leads to involvement, which leads to excellence. Make sure your team understands that failing is preferable to being fearful. If you want to build exceptional teams, teach your employees that mistakes are inevitable and that they have the capacity to transform you into something greater than you were before.

Working toward a single goal is the start of every team's advancement and a definite indicator that they're on the right track. Things start to make sense when your team learns to operate together rather than as a collection of individuals tugging in separate directions. It's remarkable what you can do when you work together to achieve a common goal. Show up as a leader and lead by example. As the leader, your own behaviour will ripple out to your team, so show up as a leader and lead by example. Make sure that what you say and what you do are in sync. Then, as a further step, encourage your team to take charge of their own leadership. Provide every team member with the opportunity to advance into an appropriate leadership position by empowering and encouraging them.

You may not always be able to provide them with all they desire, but you can constantly strive to ensure that they have what they require. Everyone works better when they are able to unwind and enjoy themselves. Fun is the ingredient that helps employees get through difficult jobs and tight deadlines, and the finest leaders know how to use it without jeopardising the team's work ethic or dedication to excellence. Make a name for yourself as a leader that people can rely on to follow through on all you say. Great leaders understand the importance of establishing a reputation for keeping their promises. It communicates to people that they can rely on you and demonstrates the type of behaviour you anticipate.

Decisions must be taken on a regular basis, and flourishing teams led by outstanding leaders understand how to act decisively and purposefully. Procrastination and perfectionism will continually slow everything down; growth and success are based on deliberate action. The finest leaders are self-assured enough to stand alone, courageous enough to make difficult decisions, and compassionate enough to listen to the concerns of others. It's difficult to grasp, yet EQ is equally as crucial as IQ. If you don't have emotional talents in hand, if you don't have self-awareness, if you can't control your stressful emotions, if you can't have empathy and have successful connections, no matter how clever you are, you won't get very far with your team or with your boss.

Encourage your team to keep going until they achieve their goals. Keep in mind that they will never be aware of their own limitations unless they are forced to confront them.Great leaders understand that pushing individuals to their limits teaches them to continually push themselves farther. When you push your limitations far enough, you find there are no limits at all. The finest teams, like the best leaders, seldom stay in the same place for long. Create several learning and growth opportunities for your team members, whether through a class, a conference, or simply a reading group or a lunchtime seminar series.

As a leader, you must model fearlessness for your team and inspire them to be courageous, take risks, and go out on a limb. Great leaders coach and teach their team because they are right there with them, not yelling and creating dread on the sidelines, but demonstrating them fearlessness and encouraging boldness. Showing your team respect and giving them a cause to admire you is the best approach to unlock greatness in them. Mutual respect is essential in every team, so lead by example and treat everyone with respect.Transparency is crucial, as is demonstrating your human side. Allow your team to recognise that being a leader does not imply having all the answers—or even trying to have them.

Instead, concentrate on inspiring everyone to achieve greatness by demonstrating the advantages of collaborative problem solving. The best way to achieve success is to find win-win solutions rather than competing with others. Everyone benefits from small victories along the way, and the greater the reward, the more possibilities you generate. Because they understand that things are continuously changing and adaptability is a crucial prerequisite for leadership, great leaders value agility and flexibility. Being an agile and flexible leader links with the requirement for your team to be collaborative and cooperative, as well as aligning and empowering teams to do so. Building a strong team necessitates developing a personal relationship with each team member. There doesn't have to be a deep friendship, but it should be a recognition that individuals are entire human beings, not just coworkers who get the job done. Spend time getting to know them and demonstrating that you actually care about them and have their best interests at heart.

When you go back, you'll have a squad that's ready to take on the world. A strong leader is truthful, and they urge their workers to be open and honest. It is critical that everyone feels comfortable speaking openly, especially when things go wrong. Honesty leads to the resolution of issues and the resolution of obstacles.Being present for your team is an important part of being a leader. Make it simple for them to contact you if they have a query or want assistance. There's no reason why your staff shouldn't be able to contact you when they need to, especially with mobile email and cell phones.

If you want a wonderful team, if you want people who are happy, you must praise, acknowledge, and praise some more. You may start reaping the benefits of your team's rising excellence once you let them know you're aware of what they can be and what they can become.True leadership entails more than just managing people. Individuals on their team are able to fulfil their full potential because of them. Being a real leader demonstrates to people that you have the ability to inspire and encourage your team for the greater success of the company. To set yourself apart as this sort of leader, you'll need to possess specific attributes that inspire your team's trust and respect. You'll go through eight criteria that will demonstrate you're a real leader in this post. True leadership is exemplified by the way you collaborate with your team to achieve your objectives. A true leader goes out of their way to help their team develop their talents so that they can attain their maximum potential. To ensure success inside the organization, they lead by example and build strong, trusted connections.

A true leader operates with integrity, which implies that they uphold ethical ideals in all facets of their lives. They should convey these principles at work in order to provide the groundwork for the actions they demand from their staff. Integrity will enable you to get respect, which will encourage your team to follow your lead. Integrity also develops your reputation in the workplace since employees will feel confident in your ability to make ethically sound judgments in any situation.

To demonstrate your professionalism at work, you should set a good example for your coworkers. Always obey organizational regulations and treat people with respect, for example. Show your staff that you care about producing high-quality work and keeping a good reputation, and they will reciprocate.

A genuine leader should strive to help his or her employees reach their utmost potential. They improve the team's potential and, as a result, benefit the organization as a whole by assisting individual members in developing their talents. Employees want to see their careers improve, so a leader who provides them with the opportunity to do so will be much more appealing.

Delegating tasks—tasks that the leader can handle themselves but that allow the allocated employees to learn something new or build certain skills—is one technique to develop personnel. You'll also profit since it frees up time for you to focus on more important or time-consuming tasks.

Allow individuals the flexibility to make their own decisions when trying to create your team. Setting boundaries and rules is necessary, but giving employees more decision-making autonomy can help them advance and feel happier in their jobs. A genuine leader should place a higher emphasis on his or her connections with his or her subordinates than on his or her position as a leader. Instead of just delegating duties to their team members, leaders should work with them to achieve this. They should take the time to get to know each member as an individual and develop deeper personal ties with them. When your team members feel valued as individuals, they will be more motivated since they will know that their efforts are respected.

When your team members finish their duties, thanking them or expressing thanks in other ways is a simple way to show your appreciation. Delivering encouraging notes is another simple way to express gratitude. For example, let an employee know after a customer presentation if you think they did a terrific job. Employees' confidence might assist them in improving their job even more when they know they're performing well at work.

A real leader must accept responsibility for their actions and expect their colleagues to do the same. They should hold themselves to a high quality of work in order to set an example for others. Recognizing your mistakes and exhibiting professional ways of recovering from them are all part of being accountable. Because everyone knows they can rely on one another to execute their jobs, creating an atmosphere that promotes accountability may boost performance and trust among team members.

Giving detailed comments on work that does not meet your expectations is one technique to create accountability in the workplace. Individuals should be spoken to clearly and gently to help them recognise their faults and how to correct them.When team members show evidence of progress, you should also applaud them. Employees will be more motivated to uphold your high standards if they feel valued and if they see you upholding them in your job. A true leader is always eager to engage in an open and honest dialogue with his or her subordinates. Being open and honest with your team builds trust, which fosters respect and a willingness to follow your example. When employees know you take the time to connect with them and tell them the truth, they feel appreciated. Make sure you speak with your team frequently, since open dialogues make everyone feel more at ease.

Aim to supply your staff with the information they require immediately to demonstrate honesty. For example, you should keep your staff informed about any organizational changes and how those changes may affect them. On a daily basis, you may demonstrate honesty by offering feedback to your team members or, if possible, conducting frequent check-ins.

A genuine leader should constantly listen to their people, both for favourable and negative feedback. Employees should be allowed to express themselves without being interrupted or judged. A good listener also tries to comprehend and sympathise with the other person's feelings and thoughts.

Make it apparent to your employees that you are accessible to listen to their problems, thoughts, and suggestions, which will make them feel valued at work and that they have a more active part in the team. Maintain eye contact and offer any clarifying questions to demonstrate that you are involved and listening during these interactions. A true leader utilises their own or the company's vision to encourage and inspire their colleagues to achieve their objectives. The leader develops a collective feeling of purpose for the team by sharing their vision with them, giving them direction and motivation. A true leader can persuade others to believe in their goal, whether by making it accessible to employees or by providing a convincing case.

Always express your clear vision to your team and make sure they understand how their roles contribute to it. When employees have a clear understanding of how they can contribute to the team's success, they will feel empowered. Establish goals for your team to achieve throughout their tasks and explain how accomplishing these goals promotes the vision. When people achieve their goals, give them good praise and support.Being brave at work might entail the capacity to be straight with your staff, in addition to demonstrating confidence in your judgments and tackling disputes. As a leader, you must make decisions that have a direct impact on your team members. You must therefore maintain confidence and bravery in your actions.

A real leader is fearless of possible conflict or criticism, especially when they know what they're doing is in the best interests of the team. Employees look up to a boss who stands up for them in any scenario. A real leader with a solid set of beliefs and a clear vision can stay fearless in the face of any obstacle.

According to recent Center for Creative Leadership research, between 38% and more than half of new leaders fail within the first 18 months of their tenure.By adopting effective leadership methods that drive their team members to achieve their goals, leaders may avoid being part of this alarming number.

While anybody may sit in a corner office and assign responsibilities, successful leadership requires more. Effective leaders have a significant influence not just on the people they supervise but also on the firm as a whole. Employees who work under outstanding leaders are often happier, more productive, and more attached to their organization, which has a positive impact on the bottom line of your company. One of the most important parts of excellent leadership is maintaining an open line of communication with your team members. "It's vital to be honest when you're in control of a group of people," he said. Your company and its employees are reflections of you, and if you put honesty and ethics first, your staff will follow suit.

"I believe a great leader is one who improves others around them," says the author.

There are several litmus tests for a great leader, but one that I look for is whether or not others around them are developing, becoming better leaders themselves, being inspired, and so on. It may be time to examine and reform your techniques if you see that your team members have grown disinterested or sluggish in their job. The following actions, according to the author, are evidence that you may have a bad leadership strategy:

- In the last month, no one in your team has questioned one of your ideas.
- You devote more attention to your own professional development than to that of your coworkers.
- You haven't had at least three non-work-related chats with a team member on a weekly basis.
- If you asked your team members what their top three priorities for the year are, they would all give you different answers.
- Members of the team are frightened of failing.

Focus on getting to know each of your team members' personalities, interests, strengths, weaknesses, hobbies, and preferences to develop a connection with them. This might help you understand their motives and ambitions.

Leaders that are successful empower their people to gain autonomy and provide value based on their own capabilities. Recognizing the skills of individuals on their team and empowering them to take responsibility and accountability boosts employee confidence in themselves and their leader, as well as their performance. Developing the shared trust essential to foster a strong culture of responsibility and excellent performance requires making genuine, human connections with your coworkers.

A leadership strategy is about empowering people to do their best and take on new challenges in order to engage and inspire personnel. Employees enjoy difficulties and the sense of accomplishment that comes with overcoming them. It's always a good idea to let them take on these obstacles, whether it's a difficult customer, a difficult sale, a difficult issue, or whatever the case may be. Leaders that trust in their staff and provide opportunities for them to learn and grow may be astonished at how much they can accomplish. Don't be scared to delegate work and promote innovation and flexibility.In my study, I've discovered that when people bring out positive aspects of a challenging scenario, they feel less passionately about it and are better equipped to think rationally and solve it. When a leader needs to strengthen their strategy, the same is true. If you or a member of your team finds that a specific course of action you've taken isn't working, think about what you've done in the past that has. Before you figure out what makes a situation unsatisfying, consider three good aspects of it. People react more positively to one another when they focus on the positive aspects of an issue.

Even though leaders wish their team's day-to-day operations ran smoothly all of the time, they're likely to hit a snag now and again. Whether it's a slight misunderstanding or a massive blunder, how you manage a difficult circumstance reveals a lot about your leadership abilities.

A more engaged and productive staff is more likely to emerge from a favourable atmosphere. A competent leader can recognise the influence they may make in their workplace by exhibiting excitement and confidence.You will not get the degree of engagement that you desire if you command individuals to perform particular things in specific ways. Coaching is about assisting those you lead in seeing the options available to them. People will then have a strong sense of ownership over the project's direction. Rather than merely giving commands to their employees, smart leaders should educate them on how to improve. People would not develop if their leaders did not teach them anything.

Leaders must teach in order to develop young leaders to take their place. Instead of merely telling others what they need to know, a good leader knows how to demonstrate it. Setting clear goals and expectations for your employees is critical to their success. Encourage employee inquiries and feedback while creating these goals. Including them in the process might help them feel more involved. Good leaders will also describe the company's vision and how individual team members' ambitions fit into that picture. A leader must keep his or her team informed about their vision in order to excite and inspire them. This helps employees comprehend the final result they're working toward as a team. Everyone can measure progress and identify accomplishments when goals are clearly defined. Don't allow team members' ambitions to become stagnant. Review your goals on a regular basis to make any necessary changes or rearrangements. This will demonstrate to your teammates that you are there and alert.

The greatest method to lead your staff in the correct direction is to give them straight, honest feedback—even if it's criticism. You must also be aware of the future direction of your company in order to provide them with sound advice. People will never know what you genuinely think about them and their work if you aren't direct, and they will never be able to improve. No matter how much you've communicated to your employees and leadership team about their individual performance, they'll fail when it comes to making decisions and taking actions if you don't know where your business is going. Deadlines, frequent product planning, performance evaluations, structure, and processes can all be simply implemented once those basic concepts are in place.

Positive reinforcement, rather than vague pats on the back, will help a person perform better in the long run. Recognizing accomplishments by detailing how they benefit the business, rather than with vague pats on the back, will help a person work better in the long run. Honest feedback is beneficial to more than just your team members. Because a real self-evaluation of your leadership is tough, mentors, fellow professionals, and even your own team may help you measure your performance. Speaking with friends and peers may help you gain valuable insight into your leadership style and approach. Leadership coaching may also assist you in identifying areas where you can improve. More inspiring than books alone might be a professional who helps you design a plan to attain your leadership goals.

Coaching enables leaders to establish the link and implement changes in the current world. You'll need time to integrate, process, and reflect, and you won't be able to make long-term changes until you go through those phases. It's worth noting that your team may provide invaluable insight into what's working, what isn't, and what roadblocks you must overcome in order to succeed. Good leaders are emotionally intelligent enough to recognise and accept the fact that change is unavoidable. Embrace change and innovation rather than striving to maintain the status quo for the sake of consistency. Be receptive to new ideas and ways of thinking. Everyone brings a distinct viewpoint to the table, which should be embraced rather than discouraged. You fully embrace every option and potential when you're open to hearing the opinions of the people around you. Persist in your efforts until the task is completed. Accept that mistakes will occur, but if something doesn't work, attempt to figure out why and how before discarding it. Encourage team members to provide their ideas while tackling a challenge. True creativity, engagement, and success can thrive when people feel free to bring fresh ideas to the table. You need the correct motivation to be a good leader. Is it about the money or the status, or do you truly want to motivate others to achieve their best?

Leadership is both an honour and a vocation for me. If you believe in your heart that leadership is your destiny and the way you'll make a difference in the world, you've come to the perfect spot. It's crucial to understand what depletes your energy, in addition to what stimulates you. Knowing your strengths and limitations allows you to broaden your team and build a well-rounded skill set. It enables you to avoid hiring carbon copies of yourself and forming friendships with people who are not like you.Your management style has an impact on how you engage with employees and should be assessed. There are nine different leadership styles, and the best leaders can adapt each to their circumstances and personnel. It's important to remember that being a good leader takes time. Although some people are born with inherent leadership abilities, it is something that anybody can learn and develop. You may lead your team to success via hard work, devotion, and smart planning.

Larry Bossidy, the famous CEO of Honeywell International, Inc., teams up with consultant and prolific author Ram Charan to discuss why getting things done is the most critical role of a corporate leader, not strategy, innovation, or anything else. The authors of this business best-seller dissect the three primary execution processes—people, strategy, and operations—and illustrate how they are intertwined. The guide to getting things done for savvy company executives is execution.

Bill George, the former CEO of Medtronic, delivers a complete leadership development programme and demonstrates how to construct your own personal leadership development plan. True North is based on personal interviews with 125 renowned leaders, including Charles Schwab, Howard Schultz (Starbucks), and Anne Mulcahy (Xerox), and explains how anybody can become a true leader by following their internal compass.

Marcus Buckingham delivers the astounding findings of Gallup's in-depth survey of more than 80,000 managers in his long-running management bestseller First, Break All the Rules. Despite their diverse backgrounds and approaches, outstanding managers have one thing in common: they aren't afraid to breach holy business conventions.

Warren Bennis, dubbed "the dean of leadership gurus" by Forbes magazine, has spent years convincingly arguing that leaders are not born, but produced. His landmark work On Becoming a Leader has served as a source of important knowledge for many readers, delving into the attributes that constitute leadership, the individuals who embody it, and the tactics that anybody can use to attain it. The call to leadership is more important than ever in a world marked by turmoil and uncertainty.

You are moved by great leaders. They stoke your fire and motivate you to be your best. When attempting to explain why they are so successful, you frequently refer to strategy, vision, or great ideas. The truth, however, is considerably more primal: successful leadership is based on emotions. Daniel Goleman, Richard Boyatzis, and Annie McKee's book, Primal Leadership, explains how managers and executives may become emotionally intelligent leaders.

The Bhagavad Gita offers a path ahead for professionals dealing with negative business karma, including overcoming self-defeating behaviours and regulating the mind's negative chatter, which is frequently the greatest impediment to successful leadership. This book gives hope for happy workplace relations and a protected environment by supporting a leadership strategy that cares for followers, stakeholders, and future generations.

There are numerous varieties of leaders, but there are fundamentally two categories: one who has the title of leader and the other who has a profession that requires leadership abilities. To be a leader, you do not need a title. A good leader is one who grooms future leaders. While much has been published about leadership, few, if any, have been written by an Indian who has walked the Indian corporate environment from field to desk to leadership. From the perspective of today's environment, this book defines true leadership. The strength of simplicity, which is based on true experiences culled from the author's own work-life, makes this book a perfect handbook for a rookie or seasoned manager.

Many of the world's life-changing technologies have come about as a result of someone failing to complete their intended purpose. He was aiming to develop a cardiac rhythm monitoring device similar to Wilson Greatbatch, the creator of the pacemaker, but he used the wrong size resistor. Wilson regarded this failure as an opportunity, which led to the development of a two-inch implanted device known as a pacemaker, which currently extends the lives of more than 500,000 people each year. As a result, embrace failure. Failure is necessary for success. Finally, innovative leaders have faith in the system. It is possible to learn how to be more creative.You may grow your own creativity or learn how to enable the creative talents of your team with enough practise, finding, and inspiration, enough sincerity to form a true team, and an awareness that failure is a part of the process. Let's assume you're interested in automotive design. You believe that automobiles must have at least four wheels in order to be safe. Then you consider what would happen if my automobile only had three wheels or none at all. This is an example of questioning your own as well as other widely held beliefs. Your design is still on three wheels, and it isn't selling.

Elon Musk is on nearly every list of business game-changers, not because he had the goals of high-speed all-electric transportation, sustainable energy, and mind-computer connections, but because he believed in them and found a means to make them a reality. With his all-electric Tesla project, he effectively flipped the automobile business on its head. With his reusable SpaceX rockets, he revolutionised the field of rocket science. He was also a co-founder of PayPal, a well-known programme, and he made his first million by selling PayPal to eBay.

Do not restrict yourself if you, too, have a desire to dream large. Allow nothing to drag you down. Leaders are not born, but made, contrary to common assumption. Of course, you'll need a little prodding to develop the correct type of leadership abilities.

Musk is a businessman, entrepreneur, and investor who was born in South Africa. Musk is most known for inventing PayPal and SpaceX, as well as his involvement with Tesla Motors. Solar power, high-speed transit, and artificial intelligence have all benefited from his vision and drive to push the frontiers of technology and consumer interaction. So, here's a toast to all the pioneering and enterprising folks who, in some way or another, have influenced others along the road. They demonstrated how to think outside the box, take chances, and stay committed to the path.

In the process, he's amassed a cult-like following on Twitter, with nearly seven times the population of New York City watching his every move. The answer is straightforward: Musk set his sights on the practically unattainable. He leads in a way that challenges what humans are capable of, whether it's founding a colony on Mars or eradicating traffic in major cities by building subterranean hyperloops that speed at 600 miles per hour. It's both inspiring and motivating to see his idea come to reality. It makes some individuals want to dig their heels in even deeper and take on the world's most difficult challenges with the same zeal. They utilize this vision to mobilise a group of individuals who believe in the importance of their cause. This aids the organisation in achieving tough goals that improve the planet. Above all, transformational leaders' organisations are driven by a sense of purpose and great outcomes.

"There have to be reasons that you get up in the morning and you want to live."-Elon Musk

Why do you want to live? What's the point? What inspires you? What do you love about the future? Really, the only thing that makes sense is to strive for greater collective enlightenment. It is important that people look forward to coming to work in the morning and enjoy working. People who are *"frequently correct"* make decisions in a unique way—how.

Power Points

- Flexibility, curiosity, investigation, and learning from so-called mistakes and failures are all required for creativity.
- A growth mindset, emphasises learning, willingness to fail, curiosity, expansion, and self-reflection.
- Leaders should focus on people's talents rather than their flaws while directing the game.
- A true leader operates with integrity, which implies that they uphold ethical ideals in all facets of their lives.

References

- *Lincoln On Leadership For Today: Abraham Lincoln's Approach to Twenty-First-Century Issues by Donald T. Phillips, Feb 2018*
- *The Leader's Companion: Insights on Leadership Through the Ages by J. Thomas Wren, Aug 1995*
- *The Edge of Leadership: A Leader's Handbook for Success by Brigette Tasha Hyacinth, Mar 2017*
- *The Leadership Crisis and the Free Market Cure: Why the Future of Business Depends on the Return to Life, Liberty, and the Pursuit of Happiness by John A. Allison, Dec 2014*
- *Leadership by Values: The Proverbial Cwtch of the Panglossian by Ramesh Subramanian, Aug 2020*
- *Leadership: Essential Selections on Power, Authority, and Influence by Barbara Kellerman, Sep 2010*
- *Tribes: We Need You to Lead Us by Seth Godin, Apr 2014*
- *Extreme Ownership: How U.S. Navy SEALs Lead and Win by Jocko Willink & Leif Babin, Nov 2017*
- *Leadership - What Really Matters: A Handbook on Systemic Leadership (Management for Professionals) by Daniel F. Pinnow, Aug 2011*
- *The Greats on Leadership: Classic Wisdom for Modern Managers by Jocelyn Davis, July 2016*
- *Transformational Leadership in Banking: Challenges of Governance, Leadership and HR in a Digital and Disruptive World by Anil k Khandelwal, Feb 2021*
- *The Leadership Challenge: How to Make Extraordinary Things Happen in Organizations (J-B Leadership Challenge: Kouzes/ Posner), Mar 2017*
- *The Spirit of Leadership: A Complete Book on Understanding Leadership by Rajendra D. Patsute, Sep 2020*
- *The Eight Paradoxes of Great Leadership by Tim Elmore, Nov 2021*
- *The Book on Leadership by John F. MacArthur, Oct 2006*

- *Inspire Your People: An Empowering Guide on Leadership from the Heart (Change Your Company: Alame Book Series) by Dr. Fouad M. Alame, Jan 2022*
- *Leaders on Leadership: Insights from corporate India (Response Books) by All Indian Management Association, Oct 2012*
- *CEO Excellence: The Six Mindsets That Distinguish the Best Leaders from the Rest by Carolyn Dewar and Scott Keller, Mar 2022-06-11*
- *The Leadership Handbook: Your Path to Growth and Success by Bomi Doctor, Nov 2020*
- *The leader in you by Dale Carnegie, Jan 2018*
- *The Only Leadership Book You'll Ever Need: How to Make Organizations Where People Love to Come to Work by Peter Barron Stark and Jane Flaherty, June 2017*
- *Leadership: Six Studies in World Strategy by Henry Kissinger, June 2022*
- *Strengths Based Leadership : Great Leaders, Teams, and Why People Follow by Tom Rath, Oct 2020*
- *Inspire Your People: An Empowering Guide on Leadership from the Heart by Dr. Fouad M. Alame, Jan 2022*
- *You, the Leader (HBR Women at Work Series) by HBR, Mar 2022*
- *Coaching: The Secret Code to Uncommon Leadership by Ruchira Chaudhary: An all-in-one Business Guide & Business Coaching Book |Business Book teaches about New Model Business, Penguin by Ruchira Chaudhary, Jan 2021*
- *Leadership Reformed: Why Leaders Need the Gospel to Change the World (Routledge Frontiers of Business Management) by Sen Sendjaya, Dec 2019*
- *Jack Welch on Leadership: Abridged from Jack Welch and the GE Way (The McGraw-Hill Books in Brief) by Robert Slater, Mar 2004*
- *A Handbook on CORPORATE LEADERSHIP | Condensed Guide for Corporate Directors & Senior Executives (New Release) by Institute of Directors India, Apr 2022*
- *Primal Leadership: Unleashing the Power of Emotional Intelligence by Daniel Goleman, Richard Boyatzis & Annie McKee, Aug 2013*

- *Leadership Strategy and Tactics: Field Manual by Jocko Willink, Jan 2020*
- *Leadership: Discover the Qualities of Leaders and How to Use Them in Your Own Life for Ultimate Success by Benjamin Smith, Dec 2016*
- *Leadership and Self-Deception: Getting Out of the Box by The Arbinger Institute, Sep 2018*
- *Leadership Interview Questions You'll Most Likely Be Asked (Job Interview Questions Series) by Vibrant Publishers, Jan 2020*
- *The Power of Positive Leadership: How and Why Positive Leaders Transform Teams and Organizations and Change the World (Jon Gordon), May 2017*
- *Impact of spiritual practices on executives' leadership behaviour by Dr. T Kumar and Dr. S. Pragadeeswaran, June 2022*
- *First, Break All the Rules: What the World's Greatest Managers Do Differently by Marcus Buckingham, May 2016*
- *Execution: The Discipline of Getting Things Done by Larry Bossidy & Ram Charan, Feb 2011*
- *The 21 Irrefutable Laws of Leadership: Follow Them and People Will Follow You by John C. Maxwell, Sep 2007*
- *True North: Discover Your Authentic Leadership by Bill George, Oct 2007*
- *Leadership IQ: A Personal Development Process Based On A Scientific Study of A New Generation of Leaders by Emmett C. Murphy, June 1996*
- *Gandhi on Personal Leadership by Anand Kumarasamy, June 2006*
- *Getting a Grip on Leadership by Robin Pearce, Lavonn Steiner, January 2012*
- *Juran on Leadership For Quality by J. M. Juran, May 2003*
- *Lessons in Leadership: 12 Key Concepts (The John Adair Masterclass Series, 2) by John Adair, Sep 2018*
- *Leadership by the Book (The One Minute Manager) by Kenneth Blanchard, Oct 2006*
- *Reflections on Leadership — My Life Experiences by G Jagannathan, Dec 2021*

- *Leading with Gratitude: Eight Leadership Practices for Extraordinary Business Results by Adrian Gostick, Chester Elton , Mar 2020*
- *The Go-Giver Leader: A Little Story About What Matters Most in Business by Bob Burg , John David Mann, July 2016*
- *Everything About Leadership by Vivek Bindra, Feb 2018*
- *100 Great Leadership Ideas by Jonathan Gifford, Aug 2019*
- *Leadership Wisdom by Robin Sharma, Nov 2003*
- *The One Thing: The Suprisingly Simple Truth Behind Extraordinary Results by Gary Keller, July 2013*
- *The Secret of Leadership: Stories to Awaken, Inspire and Unleash the Leader Within by Prakash Iyer, May 2013*
- *Start With Why: How Great Leaders Inspire Everyone To Take Action by Simon Sinek, Oct 2011*
- *The elephant at the dinner table: A journey into experiential leadership by Amit Nagpal, Sep 2021*
- *The Leadership Challenge: How to Make Extraordinary Things Happen in Organizations (J-B Leadership Challenge: Kouzes/ Posner) by James M. Kouzes, Mar 2017*
- *Leaders Eat Last (With a New Chapter): Why Some Teams Pull Together and Others Don't by Simon Sinek, May 2017*
- *The Leader Who Had No Title by Robin Sharma, Feb 2010*
- *Chanakya's 7 Secrets of Leadership by D. Sivanandhan Radhakrishnan Pillai, Jan 2014*
- *Leadership in 100 Words: Simple Tips for Complex Leadership Challenges by Mainak Dhar, Jan 2022*
- *The Leadership Pipeline: How to Build the Leadership Powered Company by Ram Charan, Nov 2010*
- *Cost of Poor Leadership: A Step-By-Step Guide to Improve Your Leadership Skills by Ramesh Kumar, Mar 2022*
- *Leadership Parables: Powerful Leadership Principles Delivered Through Simple Parables by Rajiv Chelladurai and Andy Iyer, May 2022*
- *INDOMITABLE: A Working Woman's Notes on Work, Life and Leadership by Arundhati Bhattacharya, Jan 2022-06-10*

- *My Life in Full: Work, Family, and Our Future (With a special Epilogue for India) by Indra K. Nooyi, Sep 2021*
- *Leadership Lessons from the Bhagavad Gita (Books for a Happy Work Life) by Ace Simpson, Nov 2019*
-

About The Author

Dr. Amit is the founder of Accumentors India, a consultancy firm set up by him in the human resource solution space, which is focused on developing processes for people. It offers consultancy in learning management, mentorship, performance coaching, training and development, psychometric analysis, HR processes and interventions.

Dr. Amit Das is an experienced training, and learning professional with more than 22 years of working history in the healthcare, medical devices, and learning management industries. Dr. Amit is a seasoned training professional with rich experience and a successful track record in aligning learning and training solutions to key business strategy with a strong focus on flawless execution excellence to facilitate individual, business divisional, and organisational performance. He keeps relentless focus on measuring training impact and ROI, people capability building graphs, training process governance, performance coaching, and strategic thinking. These have been some of his key individual success traits. His core capabilities include performance coaching, designing training and development frameworks and facilitation of technical skill building, psychometric assessment and analysis, competency framework development and assessments, content design and facilitation of soft skills and leadership programmes, E-Learning Platform development, Learning Management Systems, Learning Impact Measurement, Talent Analysis and Performance Management System Review, Performance Coaching and Counselling. Dr. Amit Das, is a renowned executive advisor, consultant, author, speaker and coach whose 22+ years of business experience provides high-impact, practical solutions that support his clients' leadership development and organizational transformations. Dr. Amit Das is recognized as an innovative, principled thought leader who combines intellectual rigor and discipline with an ability to translate theory into practice. His operational skills are coupled with a strategic ability to analyze, develop, and implement successful strategies for profitability, growth, and sustainability. He has been guiding people to live a better life by drawing inspiration from his own life experiences and that of others.

His interests are in the areas of leadership development, coaching competency, mentorship, and motivational complexities related to organisational issues. His hobbies include public speaking, content creation, and reading books.

He has a Ph.D. and a Fellowship in strategic learning, along with his first class degrees in Human Resource Management and Corporate Laws from the top business schools in India. He is a certified professional coach from U.K. and behavioral coach from U.S.A.

www.ingramcontent.com/pod product compliance
Ingram Content Group UK Ltd.
Pitfield, Milton Keynes, MK11 3LW, UK
UKHW021658190726
13853UKWH00001B/343